Daddy's Baby Girl . . . Forever!

A Collection of Spirit-Filled Poetry

Joyce Iona Richard Montgomery

Order this book online at www.trafford.com
or email orders@trafford.com

Most Trafford titles are also available at major online book retailers.

NIV – New International Version

Scripture taken from the Holy Bible, New International Version®. Copyright © 1973,
1978, 1984 Biblica. Used by permission of Zondervan. All rights reserved.

Print information available on the last page.

ISBN: 978-1-4907-9228-6 (sc)
ISBN: 978-1-4907-9229-3 (hc)
ISBN: 978-1-4907-9227-9 (e)

Library of Congress Control Number: 2018966061

Trafford rev. 12/18/2018

www.trafford.com

North America & international
toll-free: 1 888 232 4444 (USA & Canada)
fax: 812 355 4082

TABLE OF CONTENTS

ACKNOWLEDGEMENTS

I THANK GOD FOR SENDING MIDWIVES THROUGHOUT
MY LIFE. ALL OF YOU ASSISTED ME IN MEETING
MY DATES WITH DESTINY THUS FAR. I THANK EACH YOU
FOR ALLOWING GOD TO USE YOU IN THIS CAPACITY.
GOD USED ALL OF YOU IN MANY MIGHTY WAYS
TO BRING OUT OF ME WHAT GOD HIMSELF
DEPOSITED THAT I HAD NO IDEA EXISTED!!!

REV. LEON RANKINS, III REV. DARROLD MONTGOMERY
MINISTER KAREN MONTGOMERY
REV. ZEBEDEE NICHOLSON REV. RICK CURRY
REV. JOEY MARVIN PROPHET PAUL BRANTLEY
PROPHET ERVIN WHITLOW PROPHETESS SONJA WHITLOW
MINISTER CASSANDRA JOHNSON GREEN
MINISTER SONJA JACKSON
MINISTER KIERON COLE MINISTER O'NEIL MCRUNELLS
MINISTER NATASHA SWORD MINISTER
CARMEN ROBINSON WILSON
MINISTER ARTHUR BOYKIN CORRIE O. WINGATE
CHERYL LOVELACE POET LAMAR BROWN
MOTHER LENA WILLIAMS JEROME RANDERSON
GWENDOLYN NICHOLSON CORRIE WINGATE LEWIS
MARILYN PETERSON

DELORES MOULTRIE, ODESSA HILL, LILLIE
TOWNSEND, CECIL HUNTER, EDITH KENNEDY,
AND BOBBIE WICKER ALL TEACHERS AT BLOUNT MIDDLE
SCHOOL PENSACOLA, FL (1975-1978)

SISTER RITA O'FERRELL, SISTER MAUREN,
SISTER JANICE FATHER MOONEY, FATHER
MULLEN AND BARBARA MOBLEY ALL OF SAINT
JOSEPH SCHOOL PENSACOLA, FL (1969-1975)

I LOVE YOU ALL WITH ALL MY HEART & SOUL!

JOYCE

THIS BOOK IS FOR ANYONE WHO HAS
EVER HAD A BROKEN HEART,
ANYONE WHO HAS EVER BROKEN SOMEONE'S HEART,
ANYONE WHO HAS EVER MADE A MISTAKE
& TRIED TO FIX IT ALONE,
ANYONE WHO HAS HAD A LOVED ONE DIE,
ANYONE WHO HAS EVER BEEN LONELY,
ANYONE WHO HAS HAD TO WAIT
ON THEIR DELIVERANCE,
ANYONE WHO HAS EVER HAD SUICIDAL THOUGHTS,
ANYONE WHO HAS BEEN AT THE END OF THEIR ROPE,
ANYONE WHOSE HAS EXPERIENCED THE
TRUE MEANING OF DESPAIR,
ANYONE WHO HAS THOUGHT THEY WERE ALL
THAT ONLY TO BE REMINDED THAT THEY
WERE NOT, ANYONE WHO HAS EVER
FELT WORTHLESS AND
UNLOVABLE, ANYONE WHO HAS BEEN ACCUSE
OF SOMETHING YOU DIDN'T DO,
AND ANYONE WHO HAS BEEN CONVICTED
OF SOMETHING THEY DID DO.
I PRAY THAT YOU'LL FIND GOD,
COMFORT, KNOWLEDGE, AND POWER
THROUGH THE READING OF THIS BOOK.

DADDY'S BABY GIRL

DADDY (dad' E) NOUN-ONE WHO CREATES, ORIGINATES, OR FOUNDS SOMETHING NATURALLY OR SPIRITUALLY. INTIMATE AFFECTIONATE WORD FOR FATHER.

BABY (Ba-bE) NOUN—THE YOUNGEST OF A GROUP GIRL (g&r (-&) 1) NOUN-A FEMALE CHILD OR OFFSPRING A COLLECTION OF SPIRIT FILLED POETRY GIVEN AS A GIFT FROM GOD ALMIGHTY

BY JOYCE IONA RICHARD MONTGOMERY

PHOTO OF DADDY AND ME MARCH 1965

JUST AS YOU CAN SEE THE LOVE RADIATE FROM
THIS PICTURE OF HOW MUCH MY NATURAL
DADDY LOVED ME. THIS SHOULD GIVE YOU SOME
IDEA OF JUST HOW MUCH OUR SPIRITUAL
DADDY LOVES US ALL!!!

WHEN MY LIFE CHANGED FOREVER

Although I didn't know this scripture at the time, after all was said and done, this is what I prayed.

"My Father if it is not possible for this cup to be taken away unless I drink it, may your will be done."

Christmas day 1976 was a very exciting day for me and as it is with most eleven year olds I couldn't wait to see what gifts I had waiting for me under the Christmas tree. I awoke early that morning and I also woke up everyone else in the house. My mother, my daddy, my brother, Philip, and I gathered around the Christmas tree to see what Santa left for us. My brother Philip was eighteen, so to be quite honest I know now that everyone got up early that day because of me. I had already found out who Santa Claus really was but I pretended not to know for a few extra years for the fun of it. I had two older brothers, David, Jr., the oldest and Gerald, the second oldest. Both David Jr. and Gerald were married and had families of their own at this point. Every holiday we would all meet at my grandmother's (my mother's mom) house. Grandmother lived two houses down from us and my mother's sister lived across the street. I thought, "We must be rich because we own half the block." We always had big family gatherings at grandmother's house. All my aunts and uncles and their families would always meet together on holidays for good food and good fellowship.

Every holiday that I can remember my mother would fix my daddy a plate and she would take it to our house for him. Daddy very rarely came down to grandmother's house for these family gatherings. He always stayed home and enjoyed the football or basketball games on television while all the children in the family would go back and forward from our house to grandmother's house all day. This particular day my mother told me to ask my daddy if he was ready to eat dinner. But, being my usually silly self, I decided to play a joke on daddy. I must admit I originally did not plan to take the joke quite as far as I did. I went home and told my daddy that mother said, "She wasn't bringing him anything to eat this year and that he had to come to grandmother's house to get his dinner, if he wanted to eat!" Well, my daddy being the humble man he was, said, "Did your mother really say that?" I said, "Yes." Well, daddy believed his daddy once and I deserved that one and more. After he spanked me he told he was sorry he had to do it. His eyes were filled with tears and he told me he never wanted me to act like that again because he never wanted to spank me again. I truly believed that spanking hurt him far more than it did me, though I carried on like he was killing me. (I've always been a drama queen, too.)

Sometime prior to my daddy's death I can remember lying in my bed at night worrying about death. Many nights I lay sleepless and frightened wondering when death would come for me and all the people I loved. My episodes of obsession/depression about death began sometime in 1976. One of my earliest memories was the summer of 1976. I went to Disney World with one of my older cousins. I can remember making my daddy promise me that nothing would happen while I was gone and that everyone would be okay. I know it was GOD preparing me in his own way for the change that was to come. I believe my spirit was conscious of the near future change but my natural was uncertain to what was happening.

Well, I guess I have prolonged going to January 2,1977 long enough. That day started just like any other day. Although the end of this day took precedence to anything minute from its entrance. It was a Sunday my family went to church. Daddy stayed home because he wasn't feeling well. Daddy was not a complaining man so, if he voiced that he was not feeling well, he really wasn't feeling well. Before we left for church daddy notice that some of the neighborhood dogs had knocked over the garbage can and garbage was all over the back yard. This Sunday was a very dreary day. It was raining all day and it was quite cold for Florida. Daddy went out in the backyard to pick up the garbage the dogs had put over the yard. As he was doing this he grabbed his chest and yelled in pain. Mom went running outside to see what was wrong. He had a sharp pain but he was okay for now, it passed. Mom scolded him and told him to come in the house and lie down, and she told him we would get that trash up later. Mom asked him if he thought he should go to the hospital but he said no the pain was gone and he felt better.

We know now that the pain he felt then was the beginning of what was to come in just a few hours. What if he would have went to the hospital then? Would he still be here today? We will never know the answers to these questions but to be honest they do ponder in my mind sometimes. Daddy stayed in bed much of the day. When dark was approaching daddy grew concerned about making sure the garbage can was secure so that the dogs would not get to it again. But, that should have been the least of his worries. The garbage can was normally put on the curb in front of the house on certain days for garbage pickup. Again, momma told daddy not to go outside and mess with that garbage can because it had been raining all day. She also told him it was just too cold for him to go out tonight. Especially since he had been inside all day. My mother told daddy she would get Philip, my brother to take care of the garbage can for him. She told him not to worry about it. After mom made sure daddy was back in bed she went across the street to visit with her sister for a while.

During this time I was not at home I was at my grandmother's house. I can remember humming and skipping in the rain as I left grandmother's house for home. I reached the sidewalk, then the porch steps, and I was now on my front porch. I knocked on the door. Philip opened the door and I went in and walked all through the house. No one was in the house except Philip. I asked him, "Where is mom?" He said, "at Momma Hazel's house. Then I asked, "Where is daddy?" He said, "Taking out the garbage." I said, "The garbage can is not out." He told me daddy was probably still in the backyard while I was out front. Then I told Philip I was going to Momma Hazel's house where momma was. Philip walked me to the door to make sure I got across the street safely.

Once I got down the steps I saw daddy on the curb of the road with blood on one of his eyes. I think Philip and I saw him about the same time because right after I saw daddy, I turned to scream for Philip and he was already off the porch, down the steps, and standing next to me. Recall again, it is still cold and raining. Philip began getting daddy out of the road as cars were zooming by. I tried to help but I wasn't doing much good. I was crying and I wasn't sure what was going on. At first I thought a car hit my daddy. Philip suddenly told me to go get momma. I thought to myself, "Okay, Joyce, you can do this." Without another thought I crossed the street. I ran and I didn't even look to see if any cars were coming. I really didn't care if they were or not. I was running, screaming, and crying the whole way. When I got to my aunt's house I was banging on the door and ringing the doorbell as if I had completely lost my ever-loving mind! When the door opened I could not even make a complete sentence. Daddy, street, and blood were the only words I could get out of my mouth in between sobs.

Momma and Momma Hazel went running across the street to try and make sense of what I was trying to tell them. When they got across the street momma said, "Somebody call the ambulance." But someone who was driving by when daddy fell told us the ambulance was on the way. I think? What seemed to be hours, in all actuality were only minutes until the ambulance arrived. In the meantime daddy was fading in and out. I was screaming constantly. Mom told someone to take me in the house but I was not having that and momma was in no condition to deal with me at this point. (But under any other circumstance she would have.) I can remember daddy asking, "Is that Joyce crying? Joyce, don't cry. Joyce, please don't cry!" I said to my cousin's husband, "Do something, you work in a hospital! Don't just stand there! Save my daddy!" But there was really nothing he could do to save my daddy. He wasn't a doctor nor was he GOD. I guess I had to take it out on somebody and he was the one.

The ambulance took my daddy and it seemed as if the whole neighborhood was outside watching them take daddy away. Everyone went to the hospital to be by his side. That is, everyone except my younger cousin and me because we were too young. Grandmother did not go as well because she had to take care of us. I cried uncontrollably. My grandmother tried her best to console me as much as she could but nothing worked. I told my grandmother about the way I had been feeling for months prior. I also told her that I knew in my heart that daddy would never return home. Grandmother tried to convince me that my daddy was only 48 years old and could survive. But I told her that I was for certain daddy would surely die. I didn't mean to say it out loud but in my grief it just came out. In the days that followed, I was careful not to say it again because maybe if I didn't say it again it wouldn't come to pass I thought.

I don't remember much about Monday, January 3, 1977 or Tuesday, January 4, 1977 except going to the hospital Tuesday night with my brother and my cousins. I was actually at the hospital yet, because of my age I was not allowed to see my daddy. I was left in the lobby while the others went up to see him. The next time I saw my daddy he was lifeless at the funeral home lying in a casket. I wish they had allowed me to see him alive just one more time. That was my last chance to see him alive and I knew it was my last chance. The problem was that I couldn't convince anyone else of this without saying those dreadful words again. I asked on more than one occasion to see my daddy that night but no one felt the urgency I felt. I was so hurt but what more could I do. I was constantly told I was too young and that I would be able to see him when he was better. But I knew that was not going to happen. I questioned all my relatives who had seen my daddy. Everyone had high hopes. They all said he was doing a whole lot better and that he was sitting up. I only hoped what I knew was wrong. But I knew it was right. I knew regardless of their good reports, daddy was going to die soon but I didn't dare say it out loud, again.

I went to school January 5, 1977. When I was preparing for school mom told me she was going to the hospital to see daddy. While I was at school, I was merely going through the motions. I was in the 7th grade. During my third period class we began to watch a film. So, I propped my arms up on my desk and laid my head on my arms. Whenever we watched films at school the lights were always out in the classroom in order to see the film better. I closed my eyes briefly. When I opened my eyes I saw my daddy standing next to me in the classroom dressed in a hospital gown. He was smiling. It startled me but I said nothing and as instantly as he appeared he was gone. I was not afraid. For some reason, unknown to me at the time, I glanced at my watch and the time was 10:55 a.m. I said to myself okay it 10:55 a.m., so what! By the time I got to the next class my name was called over the intercom system. I was to come to the office and bring my things. My heart dropped so I escaped to total denial land. Because I knew the time had come and I didn't know how to handle it. So, I escaped the only way I knew how. Denial!

I went to the office and my brother was there. He checked me out of school. As we walked down the hall and out of the school he said nothing to me at all. So, as we were walking down the sidewalk to the car I said, "I'm so glad you came to get me so I can go see daddy."(Now I knew he was not there to take me to the hospital to see daddy. I was reaching for straws and not doing a good job at it.) Still he said nothing. (Now here I go again.) Then I said, "Well, how is daddy today?" He looked at me with the most terrifying expression I ever saw on his face and said, "Joyce, daddy's dead!" I said in my mind "you're a liar!" then I took off running. By the time I got to the corner he was behind me and my other brother was in front of me. My other brother came from out of nowhere. I thought he must have been waiting by the car. I said to my other brother, "HHHeee sssaaiiiddd ddaaddy wwwaass ddeeaadd! Tell him that's not true! Tell him!" He grabbed me and said, "Baby, daddy is gone!" I started screaming at both of them. I hated them for what they had just told me, as if I didn't know. But whom did I really hate? Was it they or myself? I hated myself because I knew it before it happened and there was absolutely nothing I could do to prevent it. I said to myself, "denial is not working anymore." What was I going to do? I was actually living the nightmare I had dreaded for quite sometime now. Someone whom I loved WAS dead, my DADDY!

From that point on I was never the same. I lost someone who meant the world to me. My daddy's death was absolutely devastating to me and finally, after all these years, I have finally come to terms with this ordeal. At this time GOD instructed me to share my experience with the world through this book. Daddy was, and still is, one of the driving forces in my life. Because of the unconditional love I learned and received as a child from my natural father I know without a doubt the extent of my spiritual father's love for me. The great experience of unconditional love was essential for me. It helped shape me into the person I am today, daddy's baby girl! I've learned also that my existence today depended upon that unconditional love. Take it from me GOD knows what he's doing! Sometimes GOD must put us in situation where no one else can help us effectively but him.

The period following my daddy's death was a challenging time for me. I had come to know the grips of sadness better than I could ever thought I needed to. I had bouts of depression and feelings of abandonment. And during several different low points in my entire life these same feelings would resurface. I literally saw my daddy, heard his footsteps, and felt his presence on many, many occasions after his death. As the years went by the frequency of these bizarre events gradually slowed down. Finally, at this point in my life I'm left only with my dreams and fond memories of my beloved daddy.

However, for the first six months after my daddy's death, I would shake and tremble every morning. (I now know these episodes where panic attacks.) I remember my mom holding me tight to try to stop me from having these bizarre episodes, but it was so intense that she could not make it stop. I tremble so hard it literally shook the both of us. Eventually they would subside as quickly as they began. I had no control over whatever caused these events, at least not to my knowledge. I felt my life changed forever because of one day's event and I was afraid to face another day not knowing what it would bring. As a result of what happened to my father I can remember not wanting my momma out of my sight. Momma slept with me every night for quite some time after my daddy's death. I now know my momma needed me during that point in time as much as I needed her. If momma went to the bathroom in the night and I woke up and she was not there with me I would panic. My situation had become so extreme that my mother had to awaken me and I would go to the restroom with her and stand at the door until she came out.

I never went to any counselors or should I say professionals to help me to deal with my problems. GOD was my one and only counselor and he got me through some tough times. Be encouraged. I thought I would never recover from my natural father's death and there are still some incidences that occurred during that period that I know I suppressed because of the excruciating pain. For instance, I can only remember leaving my daddy's funeral and I don't remember going to the cemetery at all. During this time, a time of complete despair, I wrote my first poem ever. I realized that writing poetry was the only positive way I could express my feelings and emotions. Had it not been for my daddy's death I might have never known about the gift of poetry GOD had deposited inside of me. It took this devastating event to bring it out. Yet, through it all GOD's grace allowed me to stay afloat and I know he will continue to sustain me.

I pray someone will find comfort in knowing I made it twenty-six years, so far, when I thought I couldn't go another step. Now, don't get the impression that everything has been honky dory for the past twenty-five years because that is just not so. GOD revealed to me that my daddy's death opened doors or should I say pathways to sin because I tried to fill my own void. GOD told me that May 5, 1981, the day I lost my virginity, came because I was trying to fill an empty piece to my puzzle with the shape of a triangle in a space fit for a circle. This error I made over and over again with all different shapes except the right one. Because of this revelation, I've learned the hard way that filling my own void is not within my power and if I try to, it will only result in failures. I am sharing this with you so you won't have to learn this the hard way. I thank GOD that my mask is removed and I can for the first time, look at the face that stares back at me in the mirror and I now understand that my pain and frustration were my introduction to the ministry HE has called me to. Failure is sometimes necessary for success. If you reflect on all so-called coincidences you will see as plain as the nose on your face that they really are not coincidences at all. You will see that they are deliberate preparation for things to come. This becomes so clear in the reflection mode. Give it a try.

GOD came through for me because I am daddy's baby girl in the natural and in the spiritual. With this proof, you should be most assured GOD would do the same for you. Understand that sometimes we're afraid to go on because of the hurt and loss but don't give up. Fear is a natural feeling of the flesh, but it is not of GOD. Just don't let fear prevent you from going on. If you experience feelings of fear that's just proof that you are human. Just keep going. If you let fear stop you, you won't get what GOD has in store for you. Be encouraged and know that GOD is right there in the midst of your situation no matter what it is. He will see you through because you are his child and he loves you more than you could ever dream possible!!! "If GOD be for you, who can be against you?" This biblical phrase can really make a difference? The answer to it is, "Nobody!"

Yes, I am a grown woman now with teenage children of my own, but sometimes without warning the eleven-year old girl inside of me resurfaces. When this happens, because of my statue and my outer appearance, it seems a bit awkward. You see, whenever I was hurting as a child all I had to do was get into daddy's arms. He would hold me and assure me everything would be fine. If he were still alive I'm sure he would give me this same comfort.

I now realize all I've ever wanted from anyone I have been involved with is for them to love me no matter what. I have wanted someone who accepts me for who I am, faults and all, yet still genuinely love and understand me. I have been a single parent for almost ten years now. My children will be grown and on their own really soon. I really need someone to spend the rest of my life with. Someone that I love and who loves me back unconditionally. Yes, since my daddy has died I've continued to grow as a whole. Each birthday I've gotten older but that eleven-year-old girl inside my thirty-eight year old body is still longing for this unconditional love in the natural, in the form of a mate, my soul mate. Is this too much to ask? I realize and thank GOD that I no longer desire this in the form of a daddy. I have a daddy in the spirit with GOD and my natural father, who I know I shall meet again. I am daddy's baby girl in the spirit and in the natural and this is an awesome experience. Why don't you give it a try!

Jonah in the belly of the fish . . .
Daddy's baby boy

Shadrach, Meshach, and Abednego in the fiery furnace . . .
Daddy's baby boys

Daniel in the lion's den . . .
Daddy's baby boy

Rehab the prostitute . . .
Daddy's baby girl

Noah in the ark during the flood . . .
Daddy's baby boy

Abraham in the new land . . .
Daddy's baby boy

Isaac on the altar . . . Daddy's baby boy

Mary the virgin with child . . .
Daddy's baby girl

Sarah and Elizabeth up in age with child . . .
Daddy's baby girls

Moses in the dessert . . .
Daddy's baby boy

Joshua in the promise land . . .
Daddy's baby boy

Joyce fatherless at eleven . . .
Daddy's baby girl

The list goes on and on. Fill in your name and your dilemma, it works for me and I'm sure it will work for you. It does not matter what it looks like. GOD has the final say, as you ARE his CHILD!!!

I cannot change the sun that shines bright up in the sky. I cannot change my date of birth or the day I'll die.
But this life brings to us choices that only we can make.

We have to be true in these choices so they cannot be made by a fake.
Some things in life we can change. Other things in life we can't
And discerning the difference between the two is part of becoming a
saint.

"WHEN DADDY SAVED BABY GIRL'S LIFE!"

PROLOGUE II

Once when I was quite young I almost innocently killed myself and my daddy snatched me from the clutches of deaths door literally, which I had opened. I was a very sheltered child and often played by myself at home. Playing alone allowed me to develop a vivid imagination and it also triggered me to be quite curious and experimental to say the least. I always joke about being so shelter as child that I only had 1 childhood disease and that was the measles. The only reason I got the measles was because it literally came to our house on transit by another child. The chickenpox did not get me until I was twenty-six years old when my children had it. But anyways, I was about five years old when this incident happened. This particular day had been especially boring to me as I was just recovering from the measles and had spent a considerable amount of time being sick and alone. When I say alone I mean there was no one to play with me. This was my first grade year in school so I had really missed going to school and being with other children. My week or so with the measles seemed an eternity. Now maybe my skin was itching or I just had too much time on my hands (I think it was the latter), but I was looking forward to taking my bath that night. Well, before bath time I had already dreamed up what I was going to get into in the bathroom. In the bathroom of the home I grew up in all the toiletries were kept on the top of the toilet back. (Where the water is stored.) When I say toiletries I mean things like deodorant, shaving cream, aftershave lotion, hair product, etc. I had a green marker that I had been writing with all day and at some point during the day decided I would take this marker apart and attempt to turn the water green at bath time. When bath time came daddy ran my bath water and when the bubbles had formed and the tub was full I went in the bathroom with the marker hidden under my clothes. (I forgot to mention I was sneaky, too.) It was in the wintertime and bath time required the heater to be on and my daddy lit the heater prior to exiting the bathroom, so I could bathe in private. Nevertheless, we had a gas space heater (the kind that had the open flame) in the bathroom. Well, immediately when I got in the tub, I experimented with the green marker and did indeed turned the bath water green. Then with the bubbles, I put them on my face like a beard. This reminded me of daddy and how he looked when he would shave his beard. (Ding, an idea popped into my head.) So I got the shaving cream off the back of the toilet and put it on my face. The razor was in the medicine cabinet. I attempted to get it but I wasn't quite tall enough to reach it. (Now for the people that have only known me as an adult, I know it really hard to picture me being short. But believe it or not I wasn't always tall.) So I improvised by using the remains of the marker as a razor and I proceeded to shave my face. After that was done I got the aftershave lotion and slapped it on my face like daddy would do. Remember I was just recovering from the measles so, when I did this it burned something awfully and it took awhile for me to get over it. In the meantime I decided to cool my burning face with some hair grease. This helped tremendously. Now since this gave me much relief and it was hair grease I decided to put some hair grease in my hair, too. When I put the hair grease back I sat it next to the spray deodorant. (Hum, I thought to my self "maybe I should play with that next.") So I picked it up and began to spray it all over the bathroom and on the open flames of the heater. As I was doing this I began to gasp for air because of the fumes that were coming from the heater as a result of the deodorant I had sprayed on it. I fell to the floor. I can recall it was easier to breathe on the floor but I knew I had to get out of there and I started to panic. Every time I stood to head for the door back to the floor I fell. I felt as if I would just faint within seconds so with only one hand I push the door slightly as that was all the strength I had. Daddy heard the door open, so he called my name. But I was unable to answer. Daddy got up and what he found was his baby girl on the bathroom floor at the door, butt-naked, hair full of hair grease, and nearly dead. He turned off the heater picked me up and took me out of the bathroom. I remember, as I was clear out of the bathroom taking the biggest breath of air I could. What a sigh of relief I felt. I thought I was a goner but daddy came to the rescue and saved me. My hero!

My spiritual daddy has saved me in the spirit and in the natural on many occasions, but one incident sticks out in my mind of how GOD gave me an illustration in the natural of what was about to happen in my life. It was August 23, 2000. I was taking my boys to school this particular morning and I made a wrong turn. When I realized I had made the wrong turn I decided I could travel across a dirt foot—path and still get to the school. (Wrong!) As I began to travel across the dirt, my car got stuck. When this happened I decided I would back up to get the car out but it only made the car sink deeper. Then the boys and me got out of the car and tried to shovel the tires out of the sand but this didn't work either. The clock was ticking, as the boys need to get to school, so I walked them to school then I went back to the car. I went into a company that was near where my car was stuck and called a tow truck. I waited there from about 8 a.m. to about 1 p.m. before the tow truck arrived. When the tow truck came, it pulled my car out of the hole, (it took about five minutes to do what I was struggling so hard with) and then I went to work.

Now it took me a few days to see what GOD was revealing to me through this incident. GOD was illustrating to me about myself in a dead end situation. (Yes, this situation was a mess I made myself!) Driving my car signified my journey in life. The wrong turn I made that morning was the wrong turn I made in life. When I realized I had made the wrong turn I kept going in this incident and in my life. My tires getting stuck in the sand was myself stuck in my situation. The tow truck taking so long to come to tow my car out is my wait for GOD to move on my behalf in my situation. Remember I waited at least five hours and I was stuck in my mess for quite some time as well. (Hum, five is the number for grace. GLORY HALLELUJAH FOR GOD'S GRACE!!!) The more I worked to get my car out of the hole the deeper the hole got. And the more I tried to get myself out of my situation the deeper I got into it. Then at last the tow truck driver came. He came and got the car keys from me, started my car, then attached their truck to my car, and then simply drove forward resulting in my car being lifted out of the sand hole that I had made. The sand began falling off my car until it was completely gone. Just as when GOD step into my predicament, he turned me around and pushed me forward with new direction and purpose. GOD got my keys, (which were the gifts he deposited in me that I had all the time) started my spiritual engine, then he attached me to him through the HOLY SPIRIT and pulled me out of the hole I had made in my life. The car was somewhat dirty and need to be washed. Just as afterwards, I was still somewhat dirty and needed to be washed. GOD cleansed me after the ordeal that I had been through then set me forth to do what I am destined to do. No matter how hard I tried to get myself out of my mess and no matter how good I thought my intentions were in doing so, I couldn't accomplish a thing until GOD stepped in. THANK YOU, GOD!!! MY HERO!

I am not a selfish person, therefore, I am honored to share Our Father (GOD) with you.

FROM NEAR TRAGEDY TO TRIUMPH (MY TESTIMONY)

I RECALL ALONG TIME AGO, I WAS
SO VERY CLOSE TO GOD.

HE WAS THERE TO GUIDE AND COMFORT ME
JUST LIKE THE STAFF AND THE ROD.

BUT SOMETHING HAPPENED I DRIFTED
OFF AND I COULD NO LONGER HEAR.

THE VOICE THAT GUIDED ME FROM MY BIRTH
THAT I HELD IN MY HEART SO DEAR.

SIN WAS THE CULPRIT THAT LED ME OUT OF
GOD'S WILL AND INTO THE WORLD.

THE DEVIL WAS NOW THE DRIVER
AND WAS TAKING ME INTO A DOWNWARD SWIRL.

SATAN WANTED ME TO THINK THAT BECAUSE
I'D FALLEN OUT OF GOD'S OWN GRACE.

THAT I HAD LOST, TOTALLY FAILED AND
SHOULD GIVE UP ON THIS RACE.

I KNOW THAT GOD DIDN'T LEAVE ME STANDING
OUT IN THE STORM AND THE COLD.

IT WAS A TRICK OF THE ENEMY THAT
SET ME UP TO FAIL AND TO FOLD.

I WAS DECEIVED AND ENTICED BY SATAN
HIMSELF BEFORE I KNEW WHAT FELL.

THE DEVIL THOUGHT HE HAD ME AND
WAS DRAGGING ME TO HELL.

GOD SENT HIS MESSENGER TO TELL
ME I COULD REDEEM MY VERY OWN SOUL.

I COULD REPENT, LEAVE MY SINS IN THE
PAST AND END UP JUST AS PURE GOLD.

I SURRENDERED MYSELF TO CHRIST HE
WASHED ME WHITER THAN SNOW.

WITH THE BLOOD OF JESUS HE WASHED
ME JUST LIKE THE BIBLE SAYS SO.

HE MOLDED ME TRANSFORMED ME TURNED
ME INTO THE PERSON YOU SEE TODAY.

ALL WASHED UP WITH THE PAST BEHIND
NO MATTER WHAT MEN SAY.

MY HORRIED PAST HAS BEEN ERASED.

AT LAST, I'M IN HIS WILL AND IN MY PLACE.

MY USED TO BE HAS FORMED THIS MINISTRY.

I WAS BROUGHT WITH
A PRICE BACK ON CALVARY.

IT'S GREAT TO BE BACK TO THE DAYS THAT
I COULD REACH OUT AND TOUCH.

MY SAVIOR, MY LORD, MY DELIVERER, MY
FRIEND AND MY CREATOR AND SUCH.

TO MY FAMILY

Each of my brothers has traits of my father. David, of course, has my daddy's name and he also has my daddy's gift to give great advice. Gerald has my father's awesome sense of stability and drive. Philip has my father's charm that will draw even the youngest child. As a child I didn't think this, but Philip, after he filled out a bit, looks like our daddy's double. In fact the only difference between Philip and my father is that Philip is taller and has a lighter skin tone. All three of my brothers have my father's ability to listen, his humbleness, his sense of being a provider, his sense of humor, his big heart, and last but not least, his charming good looks (Although, I am not the most biased on this subject).

Daddy always told my brothers, from the time I was born, that they must take good care of their little sister. Each of them has gone beyond the call of duty. Daddy truly is proud of my big brothers I'm sure. Anytime, day or night, through any kind of weather I can call on one or all of my brothers and they will come to my aide. In most families this is very rare and I love and appreciate my brothers more than they could ever know and more than I could express with words.

To my mother I say, "You have given me so much that I don't know where to begin." You are the fertile soil that has allowed me to grow into something beautiful. Thank you for teaching me how to be a dependable mother and for teaching me the importance of being a good mother. You have instilled values in me that have really taken root. You not only told me, but you showed me how to endure any kind of weather. Although you might have thought I wasn't paying any attention, you actually showed me how to keep going when storms arise. You showed me that some blows make knock you down, but you also showed me how to get up and move forward. Momma, you always quoted the bible to me as far back as I can remember. You said to me at low points in my life, "It's always darkest just before the day and that joy comes in the morning." Hearing you say these things helped me through some of the worst storms in my life. Every time I wanted to give up you and GOD wouldn't let me. I love you, Momma, with every morsel of my being.

Ta Shara, Dwight Jr., Nickolas, and Destiny, I thank GOD each day for the three most precious gifts he could have ever given me. I don't know how or why I could have made it through some ordeals in my life if it had not been for the three of you. GOD sure knew what he was doing and what I needed when he made you my children. Each of you has kept me in line that's for sure! Thank you, LORD! I could have been into all sorts of mess if being a mother wasn't so important to me. I dearly love you, Ta Shara, Dwight Jr., Nickolas, and Destiny without condition.

GERALD (LEFT), MOMMA (CENTER), PHILIP
(RIGHT) AND DAVID (FOREGROUND)
MAY 2000

I GIVE TO YOU

EVERYTHING THAT MATTERS, LORD,
I GIVE IT ALL TO YOU.
ALL THE THINGS I FIND APPEALING
ON LIFE'S ENTICING COURSE MENU.

OH TASTE AND SEE THAT THE LORD IS GOOD.
HE WHO TAKES REFUGE IS BLESSED. BECAUSE
IN PROTECTING AND PROVIDING
GOD YOU ARE THE VERY BEST.

MY MOTHER TO YOU I GIVE SIMPLY
BECAUSE I LOVE HER SO.
KEEP HER CONSTANTLY IN YOUR CARE AND
ALL YOUR GRACE ON HER BESTOW.

TAKE MY CHILDREN, DEAR LORD, BUILD A
FENCE TO KEEP THEM FROM ALL HARM.
THEN CRADLE THEM WITH YOUR MIGHT AND
KEEP THEM SAFE IN YOUR LOVING ARMS.

MY DEAR BROTHERS AND THEIR FAMILIES KEEP WATCH
OVER THEM DAY AND NIGHT. KEEP THEM IN YOUR ARK
OF SAFETY AND DON'T LET THEM OUT OF YOUR SIGHT.

FOR MY DEAR, SWEET, LOVING, AND FAITHFUL
HUSBAND WHOM I DON'T HAVE WITH ME YET.
TAKE CARE OF HIM ON HIS JOURNEY AS
OUR DATE WITH DESTINY IS SET.

FOR ALL MY FRIENDS AND RELATIVES MAKE CERTAIN
THEIR NEEDS ARE PROVIDED. AND WITH YOU THEIR
CHOICE FOR ETERNITY HAS ALREADY BEEN DECIDED.

LORD, BLESS ALL OF US
AND INCREASE EACH OF OUR TENTS.

AND IF WE FALL SHORT OF YOUR GLORY
REMIND EACH OF US TO REPENT.

GOD BLESS THE SICK, ALL THAT ARE IN HOSPITALS,
MENTAL INSTITUTIONS, AND PRISON ON THIS
EARTH. SHOW THEM YOUR STRENGTHS AND
POWERS THEN MOST OF ALL YOUR WORTH.

LORD BLESS THE CHURCH, IT IS YOURS
ALREADY JUST AS EVERYTHING ELSE ON MY
LIST. GLORY BE TO THE ONLY LIVING GOD
AND I SEAL THIS PRAYER WITH A KISS.

JUST IN CASE

JUST IN CASE I DON'T LIVE AS
LONG AS I THINK I SHOULD.
JUST IN CASE GOD CALLS MY NAME
SOONER THAN I THOUGHT HE WOULD.

REMEMBER I'M NOT PERFECT
NOR AM I AN ANGEL FROM HEAVEN ABOVE,
BUT I DID ACCEPT GOD'S PLAN
AND MOST OF ALL HIS LOVE.

EVERYDAY I TRIED TO BE A BIT
BETTER THAN I WAS THE DAY BEFORE.
I DIDN'T MAKE EVERYONE HAPPY.
MY NAME ALL DID NOT ADORE.

THERE IS NOTHING I WOULDN'T DO FOR
YOU FOR A LONG OR LITTLE WHILE.
WITHOUT SHOES FOR YOU I WOULD WALK
A LONG, HOT COUNTRY MILE.

JUST IN CASE I NEVER SAID
OR SOMEHOW YOU NEVER KNEW.
THE HAPPIEST DAY OF MY LIFE WAS
THE DAY I LAID EYES ON YOU!

JUST IN CASE I'VE GONE ON AND
YOU WONDER HOW I FELT.
JUST IN CASE YOUR MIND
PLAYS TRICKS AND ALL YOUR MEMORIES MELT.

GOD GAVE YOU TO ME AS A GIFT
TO HIM I GAVE YOU BACK.
I DID THIS SO YOU MAY PROSPER
AND NEVER BE IN LACK.

LEARN SOMEHOW FROM MY MISTAKES

SO MY LIVING WILL NOT BE IN VAIN.
I SHARED MY MISHAPS WITH YOU SO
YOU WON'T HAVE TO FEEL MY PAIN.

GOD BLESS AND FOREVER KEEP YOU
INSIDE HIS PROTECTIVE FENCE.
HE WILL FIGHT YOUR BATTLES FOR YOU
AND WILL COME TO YOUR DEFENSE.

JUST IN CASE I NEVER SAID
OR SOMEHOW YOU NEVER KNEW.
THE HAPPIEST DAY OF MY LIFE WAS
THE DAY I LAID EYES ON YOU!

I DID HAVE FOUR EXCEPTIONAL DAYS
EVEN IF I HAD NO MORE.
THE TITLE MOTHER MEANT SO MUCH
AND IS THE BEST I EVER WORE.

THE GREATEST LOVE OF ALL IS THE LOVE
SHARED BETWEEN A PARENT AND CHILD.
THE MERE MENTION OF YOUR NAMES WERE
ENOUGH TO MAKE ME SMILE.

JUST IN CASE I NEVER SAID
OR SOMEHOW YOU NEVER KNEW.
THE HAPPIEST DAYS OF MY LIFE WAS
THE DAY I LAID EYES ON EACH OF YOU!

DEDICATED TO MY BABIES

TASHARA, DWIGHT JR., NICKOLAS, AND DESTINY
PENSACOLA, FL

TASHARA (AGE 3), DWIGHT JR (AGE 18 MONTHS)
AND NICKOLAS (AGE 2 MONTHS)
JANUARY 1988

THE HOLY GHOST

CATCH THE SPIRIT WHILE IT'S MOVING
IT'S ALL OVER THE PLACE.
ONCE YOU GET IT, YOU WON'T BE
SATISFIED WITH JUST A TASTE.

YOU MUST BE FORGIVEN
HOLY, CLEAN, AND PURE.
FOR THE SPIRIT TO MANIFEST, I TELL
YOU THIS CAUSE I'M SURE.

YOU ARE THE PROMISE
FROM THE BLESSED FATHER.
HEAVEN SENT YOU'RE GOD'S
HOLY MESSENGER.

THE SPIRIT FORMS OPINIONS, CHANGES
ATTITUDES AND CUTS LIKE A KNIFE.
THE SPIRIT WILL DWELL INSIDE OF YOU
AND TRANSFORM YOUR ENTIRE LIFE.

EVERYTHING YOU DO NOT NEED
WILL BE REPLACE WITH GOOD.
THE HELPER WILL GIVE YOU POWER
WHEN YOU DIDN'T KNOW YOU COULD.

YES, IT'S JUST LIKE FIRE
SHUT UP IN YOUR BONES.
THIS REBIRTH WILL PUT YOU IN
BRAND NEW SPIRITUAL ZONES.

HOW DID YOU LIVE WITHOUT IT
YOU WILL SURELY ASK YOURSELF.
YOU'RE AN HEIR TO THE KINGDOM
AND HAVE COME INTO YOUR WEALTH.

I DIDN'T KNOW LIFE
COULD BE SO SWEET
I DIDN'T KNOW THE TONGUES
I BEGAN TO SPEAK.

THE HOLY GHOST TRANSFORMED ME
RIGHT BEFORE MY VERY EYES.
THE HOLY GHOST IS REAL
AND IT SURELY CHANGES LIVES

MY BROTHER'S KEEPER

HOW MANY MUST DIE BEFORE WE STAND
TO BE OUR BROTHER'S KEEPER.
HOW CAN WE SIT BY AS IF TO LET HIM
FALL WOULD BE MUCH CHEAPER.

NO MATTER WHAT THE COST IN DOLLARS
OR THE TIME IN HOURS IT TAKES.
YOU ARE YOUR BROTHER'S KEEPER SO
ACT LIKE IT FOR GOODNESS SAKE.

HOW MANY MUST DIE BEFORE SOMEONE
WILL STEP UP TO THE PLATE.
IT COULD BE YOU NEEDING HELP TO
WASH AND CLEAN YOUR SLATE.

EVEN IF YOUR BROTHER DOESN'T SEEM TO
LISTEN GO AHEAD AND PLANT THE SEED.
IT WILL TAKE ROOT AND GROW
THEN MANIFEST AT IT'S OWN SPEED.

HOW MANY MUST DIE BEFORE WE TAKE
BACK WHAT IS ACTUALLY OURS.
YOU ARE MORE THAN A CONQUEOR AND IN
YOUR HANDS GOD PLACED THE POWER.

TO TREAD OVER SERPENTS WITHOUT
THE FEAR OF BEING BITTEN.
YOU ALREADY KNOW THIS AS IN
THE BIBLE THIS IS WRITTEN.

SO EVEN IF ALL YOU CAN DO, IS KEEP
YOUR BROTHER LIFTED IN PRAYER.
INTERCEED, STAND IN THE GAP,
BECAUSE YOU TRULY CARE.

HOW MANY MUST DIE FROM GOING
ASTRAY AND WE JUST SIT BACK AND LOOK.
LIKE SLAUGHTERED MEAT SATAN CAPTURES
OUR BROTHERS AND HANGS THEM ON A HOOK.

WE KNOW WE SHOULD TRAVEL THE ROAD
THAT'S OF THE STRAIGHT AND NARROW.
WE KNOW GOD LOVES US BECAUSE
HE EVEN WATCHES THE SPARROW.

SOMETIMES WE ARE ENTICED AND END
UP OUT OF GOD'S OWN WILL.
THAT'S WHEN A BROTHER'S KEEPER
GOES TO GOD FOR US TO KNEEL.

NOT ONE MORE BROTHER SHOULD DIE
WITHOUT US PUTTING UP A DECENT FIGHT.
EVEN IF WE MUST INVADE HIS SPACE AND
NOT LET HIM OUT OF OUR SIGHT.

JUST THAT EXTRA EFFORT
MAY CAUSE HIM SOME SMOTHERING STRIFE.
BUT IT JUST MAY BE ENOUGH TO
SAVE OUR BROTHER'S LIFE.

STRONG BLACK BROTHERS

I SALUTE MY STRONG BLACK BROTHERS
ON A JOB WELL DONE.
YOU ARE RARE, FAR BETWEEN IN
MY BOOK SECOND TO NONE.
YOUR WIVES ARE PROUD
YOUR MOMS BRAG AND BOAST.
ABOUT HOW THEY RAISED A MAN
THAT'S BETTER THAN MOST.
YOU PRAY FOR YOUR FAMILIES
PROVIDE FOR THEM, TOO.
FOR THEM THERE IS NOTHING YOU WOULD NOT DO.
YOU ARE A STRONG BLACK MAN
THAT KNOWS HOW TO ACT.
IN THAT DEPARTMENT
YOU TRULY DON'T LACK.
LARGE IN STATUE
MIGHTY AND BOLD.
YOU ARE THE HEAD
OF YOUR HOUSEHOLD.
WHEN YOU LOOK IN THE MIRROR
I KNOW WHAT YOU SEE.
A TALL HANDSOME MAN
BEING ALL HE CAN BE.
YOUR LEGACY WILL STAND TALL
LONG AFTER YOU ARE GONE.
YOUR HARVEST WILL BE GRAND
BECAUSE OF THE SEEDS YOU'VE SOWN.
YOU WERE MADE IN GOD'S OWN
IMAGE, THIS I CAN TELL.
YOUR SPIRIT WON'T ALLOW YOUR
EGO TO EVEN START TO SWELL.
HANDLE YOUR BUSINESS MY DEAR
BROTHERS FOR WE LOOK UP TO YOU.
IT WILL TAKE SOMEONE BETTER
THAN BEST TO WALK IN YOUR SHOES.
I SALUTE MY STRONG, BLACK BROTHERS

ON A JOB ABSOLUTELY WELL DONE.
REMARKABLE, OUTSTANDING WITH NO
DOUBT SECOND TO NONE.

DEDICATED TO MY BIG BROTHERS

DAVID RICHARD, JR., GERALD RICHARD,
SR., AND PHILIP RICHARD
PENSACOLA, FL

SINFUL FOR A SEASON

HE LOOKS BEYOND MY FAULTS
BUT USES ME ANYWAY.

WHY ME LORD I'M NOT WORTHY
YET, I'LL DO JUST WHAT YOU SAY.

LORD YOU KNOW I HAVEN'T ALWAYS
BEEN GOOD AND WAS IN YOUR PERFECT WILL.

ARE YOU SURE I AM THE ONE FOR THIS
THIS CHARGE TO KEEP AND FULFILL?

I AM SORRY FOR THIS QUESTION AS I
KNOW YOU'VE SEEN WHAT I'VE DONE.

ALL THE TIME I KNEW YOU WERE
CALLING BUT I DECIDED TO RUN.

BEFORE YOU TOUCHED MY SOUL I WAS
SO LOST IN THIS SINFUL LAND.

I HAD SUNK INTO SATAN'S TRAP SO DEEP
MY HEAD WAS BURIED IN THE SAND.

I KNEW MY GOD WAS ABLE SO
I PRAY FOR HIM TO PULL ME OUT.

GOD DID JUST WHAT I ASKED CAUSE
IN MY HEART I HAD NO DOUBT.

HE WASHED ME UP ON THE OUTSIDE
THEN HE WASHED ME DEEP WITHIN.

HE MADE MY JAGGED EDGES SMOOTH
AND MY DISCERNMENT AS SHARP AS A PIN.

HE PENETRATED THE HOLY SPIRIT INTO
THE ESSENCE OF MY SOUL.

I AM A BRAND NEW CREATURE
NOTHING LIKE THE DAYS OF OLD.

HE LOOKS BEYOND MY FAULTS
AND USES ME ANYHOW.

NEVER AGAIN WILL SATAN HAVE
ME AS I KNOW I BELONG TO GOD NOW.

I AM SO GLAD HE DUG ME UP FROM WAY
BENEATH THE GRAVEL.

I'M TIED UP, SOWN UP, WRAP UP
AND WILL NEVER BE UNRAVELED.

LORD, IF YOU WANT ME TO SING
I'LL SING MY HEART OUT JUST FOR YOU.

LORD IF YOU WANT ME TO PREACH, I'LL SPREAD
YOUR WORD THE REST OF MY LIFE THROUGH.

IF YOU WANT TO USE MY HANDS TO
WORK MIRACLES IN YOUR NAME.

I WILL DO JUST WHAT YOU ASK YOUR
GRACE AND GLORY I SHALL PROCLAIM.

I OWE MY ALL AND ALL TO
MY FATHER UP ON HIGH.

I DON'T KNOW HOW HE LOVES ME
I REALLY DON'T KNOW WHY.

I HAVE NEVER BEEN PERFECT
BUT I'M STRIVING EVERYDAY.

I GIVE HIM ALL THE GLORY
WHEN I BOW MY HEAD TO PRAY.

HOW GREAT THOU ART MY SAVIOR
WHO RESCUED ME FROM SIN.

I AM NOW SANCTIFIED AND HOLY
REGARDLESS OF WHERE I'VE BEEN.

THE UNLIKELY CANDIDATE

WHEN GOD PICKS A CANDIDATE
TO CARRY OUT HIS WILL.
THE ONE THAT SOARS LIKE AN EAGLE MAY
NOT BE THE ONE FOR THIS JOB TO FILL.

THE GLORY BELONGS TO GOD AND
HE WILL DEFINITELY NOT SHARE.
HONOR AND MAJESTY ARE HIS WARDROBE
AND ARE ONLY FOR HIM TO WEAR.

HE MAY REALLY NEED SOMEONE WHO
HAS BEEN DOWN AND OUT BEFORE.
OR SOMEONE HE HAS RESCUED FROM
THE CLUTCHES OF DEATH'S DOOR.

HOW CAN YOU MINISTER TO PEOPLE ABOUT
SOMETHING YOU REALLY DON'T KNOW.
EXPERIENCE COME FROM WHAT YOU DID WHEN
YOUR CLOUDS AT ONCE HUNG LOW.

BELIEVE ME, YOU DON'T GO THROUGH SOMETHING
FOR THE SAKE OF GOING THROUGH.
YOUR TESTIMONY IS TO HELP SOMEONE
OUT OF THE SAME MESS YOU USED TO DO.

TO SAVE JUST ONE SOUL FROM DESTRUCTION
IS WORTH ALL THE HURT AND PAIN.
THIS USES THE DEVIL'S OWN STUFF AGAINST HIM
AND WILL DRIVE HIM COMPLETELY INSANE.

WE ARE ON THE BATTLEFIELD IN THE
WAR BETWEEN DARKNESS AND LIGHT.
BECAUSE WE ARE CHILDREN OF THE KING
WE HAVE NO CHOICE BUT TO FIGHT.

THE BATTLE IS NOT YOURS ALONE IT
BELONGS TO THE GREAT ONE ABOVE.
WHO SHOWERS US WITH MERCY
AND GIVES US ALL HIS LOVE.

DON'T ACCEPT THE LABELS OF THE WORLD
NO MATTER WHAT THE KIND.
MAKE FOR CERTAIN THAT FROM
GOD YOU ARE DELIVERED, SEALED, AND SIGNED.

PRAY

PRAY AND ASK GOD FOR
ANYTHING YOU NEED.
HE IS FAITHFUL AND WILL BE
THERE FOR YOU YES, INDEED.

FOR ALL YOUR BURDENS YOU SHOULD
TAKE AND LEAVE THEM AT HIS FEET.
PLEASE DON'T GO BACK TO GET THEM
AS YOU WILL SURELY MEET DEFEAT.

AS THE BIBLE TELLS US WE HAVE
NOT BECAUSE WE DIDN'T INQUIRE.
CALL ON THE ALMIGHTY, WHENEVER, HIS
GRACE AND MERCY I ALWAYS ADMIRE.

IF YOU ARE GOING TO WORRY
DON'T PRAY JUST BE DEPRESSED.
IF YOU ARE GOING TO PRAY DON'T WORRY
AND REAP THE BLESSED SUCCESS.

THE ULTIMATE POWER

WE MUST FIRST ACCEPT THAT NOTHING HAPPENS
BECAUSE OF US, WE HAVE NEVER BEEN IN CHARGE.

WE MUST ADMIT THAT WE WOULD BE UTTERLY LOST
WITHOUT GOD'S GLORIOUS PRESENCE AT LARGE.

GOD IS ABLE TO ACCOMPLISH HIS PERFECT WILL
REGARDLESS TO OUR IMPERFECTIONS.

HE IS WILLING TO GET US OUT OF ANY CIRCUMSTANCE
BUT WE MUST OBEY HIS DIRECTIONS.

REGARDLESS OF WHAT WE'VE DONE
OR ANY FOOLISH PAST DECISIONS.

IF WE ASK FOR FORGIVENESS
HE WILL GIVE WITH THE DEEPEST COMPASSION.

GOD IS IN CONTROL OF ALL THAT GOES ON
DURING OUR LIFE'S CYCLE THROUGH.

SO BE WISE, PUT HIM FIRST IN ALL THINGS
AND ACKNOWLEDGE HIM IN WHATEVER YOU DO.

THE CHANGE

IF YOU'VE BEEN REDEEMED AND YOU
KNOW IT SHOW SOME SIGN!
THIS BEHAVIOR SHOULDN'T BE HARD
IF YOUR TESTIMONY IS GENUINE.

IF YOU ARE SAVED THERE WILL BE A DRASTIC
CHANGE IN THE WAY THINGS ARE HANDLED.
YOU WILL BE SO MOUNTED IN YOUR BELIEFS
TO YOU THEY CAN'T HOLD A CANDLE.

LIKE A TREE PLANTED BY THE WATER
UNMOVABLE BY ANY STRONGHOLDS.
INFLUENCED BY NOTHING THE WORLD
CAN OFFER YOU'RE FREE IN GOD AND BOLD.

YOU WILL DEMONSTRATE THE TRUE
CHARACTERISTICS OF A CHILD OF THE KING.
AN UPRIGHT HEIR TO THE PROMISES
THE LORD WILL SURELY BRING.

OFFER YOUR BODIES AS A LIVING
SACRIFICE HOLY AND TO GOD SO PLEASING.
WORLDLY TENDENCY LIKE ALL THE
UNGODLY YOU ARE TOTALLY SEIZING.

DO YOUR BEST TO PRESENT YOURSELF
TO GOD AS ONE STAMPED APPROVED.
WHERE GODLESS CHATTER IS CEASED AND FROM
YOUR VOCABULARY IS REMOVED.

LET YOUR LIGHT SHINE BEFORE MEN THAT
THEY MAY SEE YOUR GOOD WAYS.
SO THAT TO YOUR FATHER IN HEAVEN MEN
WILL GIVE HIM ALL THE PRAISE.

MAKE SURE YOU KEEP YOUR ANOINTING FRESH
SO IT WILL NEVER LOOSE ITS FLAVOR.
MAKE IT A RITUAL EVERYDAY TO
BASK IN GOD'S HOLINESS TO SAVOR.

FOR IF YOUR ONLY MISSION IS TO LOOK
AFTER ONLY YOURSELF, YOU WILL NEVER SEE.
BUT IF YOU LOOK TO JESUS ONLY
YOU WILL FIND YOURSELF AND THEE.

GRANDMA'S BITTER CUP

MY GRANDMA TOLD ME ONCE, "IT'S NOT NATURAL
TO TO OUT LIVE YOUR CHILD.
AS TEARS FELL FROM HER EYES I PONDERED
HER EXACT WORDS FOR QUITE AWHILE.
IT MUST BE VERY DEVISTATING TO SEE WHO YOU
GAVE BIRTH JUST PASS AWAY.
YOU ALWAYS THINK THEY'LL BE THE ONE
CRYING AT YOUR GRAVE ON THAT DAY.

SOMETIMES THE TABLES TURN IT'S YOUR HEART
THAT GETS THE CRUSH.
THE LOSS YOU THOUGHT YOU'D NEVER FEEL
BECOMES YOUR CHEEK THE TEAR DOES BRUSH.
BOTH MY GRANDMAS FELT THIS PAIN TWICE
BEFORE THEY WENT TO REST.
THEY TRIED TO CARRY ON SOMEHOW
THEY REALLY DID THEIR BEST.

HOW I HATED TO SEE THOSE TEARS FALL
FROM SUCH A LOVING FACE.
I DIDN'T KNOW WHAT TO DO IN HER
HEART I COULDN'T TAKE THEIR PLACE.
THERE IS NO OTHER PERSON WHO COULD TAKE
THE PAIN FROM MY GRANDMA'S HEART.
SO SHE HAD TO TAKE IT WITH HER WHEN
SHE CLOSED HER EYES FROM EARTH TO PART.

THINGS FOR HER WERE NOT THE SAME
AS SHE WALKED CLOSER TO DEATH'S DOOR.
SHE KNEW SHE SOON WOULD HAVE TO CROSS
AND THIS PAIN WOULD BE NO MORE.

THE MEMORY OF THIS CHILD WILL
LIVE ON AND NEVER DIE.
BECAUSE A PRECIOUS GIFT THEY ARE
AND THE TWINKLE IN HER EYE.

SHE REMEMBERED SHE WOULD SEE THIS CHILD
WHEN WE ALL MEET IN THE AIR.
UNTIL, THEN THEY ARE WELL PROTECTED
WITHOUT A PAIN, WORRY, OR A CARE.
SO, IF YOU EVER EXPERIENCE THIS
AND YOU DON'T KNOW WHAT TO DO.
GOD SAYS, "THERE IS COMFORT IN
KNOWING I SAW MY CHILD DIE, TOO."

IN LOVING MEMORY OF MY GRANDMOM

LOLA WHITING WINGATE
PENSACOLA, FL
JUNE 16, 1902-JANUARY 12, 1988

JUST BE WHO YOU ARE

SOME GIRLS WEAR DRESSES,
MOST BOYS WEAR PANTS.
SOME BOYS PLAY FOOTBALL
MOST GIRLS LIKE TO DANCE.
SOME GIRLS ARE QUITE PRISSY
DRESSED ALL UP IN LACE.
SOME BOYS ARE TOUGH
AND LOVE TO RACE.
SOME GIRLS WEAR OVERALL
AND SOME BOYS DO, TOO.
IF YOU GO STRICTLY BY THE RULES
YOU WON'T KNOW WHO'S WHO.
EVEN THE GIRLIEST GIRL MAY
LIKE PLAYING WITH THE BOYS.
AND THE TOUGHEST BOY
MAY ENJOY PLAYING WITH GIRL TOYS.
THE GIRL WHO PLAYS WITH THE BOYS
WILL LEARN TO COPE WHEN LIFE GETS ROUGH.
AND THE BOY WHO PLAYS WITH DOLLS
WILL LEARN ABOUT DADDY STUFF.
THIS IS WHY BOY/GIRL RULES
ARE NOT CARVED IN STONE
IMPORTANT LESSONS ARE LEARNED
DIFFERENT WAYS I HAVE SHOWN.
SOME GREAT CHEFS ARE MEN
SO BOY GO ON AND BAKE.
GIRLS IF YOU WANT YOU CAN
CATCH FISH IN THE LAKE.
THERE IS NOT A SET STANDARD
THAT A CERTAIN GENDER MUST FOLLOW.
LIVE EACH DAY TO THE FULLEST
AND DON'T FRET ABOUT TOMORROW.
MOST IMPORTANTLY JUST BE
EXACTLY WHO YOU ARE.
THE SKY IS THE LIMIT YOU CAN
REACH FOR THE HIGHEST STAR.

GOD IS OUR CREATOR SO WHAT OTHERS
SAY DOESN'T MEAN A THING.
YOU CAN BE WHATEVER YOU WANT
BECAUSE YOU'RE CHILD OF THE KING.
WHETHER A BOY OR GIRL YOU ARE
QUITE PRECIOUS IN HIS SIGHT.
IN ALL THINGS DO WHAT YOU
KNOW IN YOUR SPIRIT IS RIGHT.

DEDICATED TO MY BABY GIRL

DESTINY MONTGOMERY, AGE 3, 2003

STAY AHEAD

BE ONE STEP AHEAD OF THE DEVIL AND
STOP HIM DEAD IN HIS TRACKS.

BE ONE STEP AHEAD OF THE DEVIL HE KNOWS YOUR
WEAKNESS AND ALL THAT YOU LACK.

BE ONE STEP AHEAD OF THE DEVIL
HE WILL CONSUME YOU AND TAKE ALL YOUR KEYS.

HE WILL USE YOUR DISABILITIES AS STEPPING
STONES TO CUT YOU OFF AT THE KNEES.

BE ONE STEP AHEAD OF THE DEVIL, HE IS
EMPEROR ONLY IN HIS OWN MIND.

BE ONE STEP AHEAD OF THE DEVIL, HE'S
TRYING TO ROB GOD OF ALL MANKIND.

BE ONE STEP AHEAD OF THE DEVIL, AS HE IS
GOING TO MAKE IT DIFFICULT FOR YOU.

BE ONE STEP AHEAD OF THE DEVIL AND
BE SURE TO DO THE SAME FOR HIM, TOO.

BE ONE STEP AHEAD OF THE DEVIL
HE IS FULL OF MISCHIEF AND GRIEF.

HE WILL COME INTO YOUR HOME AND TAKE OVER
HE IS NO BETTER OFF THAN A THIEF.

BE ONE STEP AHEAD OF THE DEVIL AND
PUT YOUR FOOT RIGHT ON HIS NECK.

BE ONE STEP AHEAD OF THE DEVIL, IF YOU DON'T
IT WILL BE YOUR LIFE HE'LL WRECK.

BE ONE STEP AHEAD OF THE DEVIL
BECAUSE HE IS THREATEN BY YOU.

BE ONE STEP AHEAD OF THE DEVIL AND
SOMETIMES YOU WILL HAVE TO BE TWO.

DON'T TAKE HIS MARK!

IF SOME LOVED ONES VANISH,
ALL BABIES, AND UNBORNS, TOO.
YOU CAN REST ASSURE IT
WAS THE RAPTURE.
IF YOU ARE STILL HERE, YOU
KNOW WHAT THAT MEANS.
YOU HAVE SET YOURSELF
UP TO BE CAPTURED.
NOW SATAN WILL TRY
TO TRAP YOU BUT STAND
YOUR GROUND NO MATTER
HOW LOUD HE BARKS.
NO MATTER THE FEAR OR
THE PLEASURE HE PROMISES
REMEMBER PLEASE DON'T
TAKE HIS MARK!

BELIEVE ME, HE WILL PROMISE
YOU JUST ABOUT ANYTHING
TO GET YOU
TO COME TO HIS SIDE.
AND IF YOU FALL PREY TO
HIS DEVIOUS SCHEMES
THEN YOU WILL KNOW
HE SURELY LIED.
NOW SATAN WILL TRY
TO GET YOU
HE WANTS TO KEEP
YOU TOTALLY IN THE DARK.
NO MATTER THE FEAR OR THE
PLEASURE HE PROMISES
REMEMBER, PLEASE DON'T
TAKE HIS MARK!

IF YOU FIND YOURSELF LEFT BEHIND AND
YOU DON'T KNOW WHICH WAY TO TURN.
I LEAVE YOU THIS MESSAGE,
AS I DON'T WANT YOU TO BURN.
YOU THOUGHT HE TORMENTED YOU IN
THE PAST, BUT YOU AIN'T SEEN NOTHING YET.
PLEASE JUST DO WHAT I ASKED
AS JESUS HAS PAID YOUR DEBT.
HEAVEN IS AWESOME AND FULL OF BLISS.
HELL IS DISGUSTING WITH A SMOTHERING MIST.
THIS IS MY LAST WARNING. PLEASE TAKE HEED!
IT WON'T BE A DAY IN THE PARK.
IF YOU CAN'T RECALL ANYTHING ELSE
REMEMBER, PLEASE DON'T TAKE HIS MARK!

CREATION OF BEAUTY

I TOOK THE TIME TO SIT BACK AND SEE ALL
THE BEAUTY GOD PUT ON THIS EARTH.
HAVE YOU EVER THOUGHT OF ITS VALUE OR
PUT AN AMOUNT ON ITS WORTH?

THE SPARKLING STAR, THE ENCHANTING MOON, OR THE
AUTUMN TREE, WHAT A GLAMOROUS SIGHT IT POSSESSES.
THE GRASS SO GREEN, THE CLEAR BLUE SKY AND
LET'S NOT FORGET ALL THE THINGS GOD BLESSES.

NOT ONLY DID I SEE GOD'S CREATION OF BEAUTY
I HEARD IT JUST AS PROFOUND.
SMALL AND LARGE NOISES FROM ALL CREATURES
IT WAS AN ARRY OF ALL DIFFERENT SOUNDS.

IN THEIR OWN TONGUE THEY
GAVE GOD HIS DUE PRAISES.
HE UNDERSTOOD EACH ONE AS
THE MASTER IS QUITE AMAZING.

NOW SINCE I HAVE BROUGHT HIS
BEAUTY TO YOUR ATTENTION.
GIVE HONOR AND THANKS IN YOUR
PRAYERS YOU SHOULD MENTION.

THE MASTER'S WILL

I AM NOT ON TRIAL BECAUSE GOD
HAS CALLED ME TO PREACH.
MY TESTIMONY SHOULD PROVE TO YOU
JUST HOW FAR OUR GOD WILL REACH.

GOD'S GRACE CAN COVER A
MULTITUDE OF SIN.
OH YES, IT IS SUFFICIENT
AND YOU NEED NOT TO DEFEND.

THERE IS A DIFFERENCE FROM BEING UNBLEMISHED
VERSES BEING COVERED BY THE MASTER'S WILL.
THE CONTRAST IS SIMILAR TO
FANTASY VERSES WHAT WE KNOW IS REAL.

INSTEAD OF YOUR EXPECTATIONS
JUST ASK FOR WHAT IS YOURS.
WE DON'T REALLY DESERVE ANYTHING,
BUT IF YOU'RE HUMBLE GOD WILL UNLOCK DOORS.

WHAT YOU THINK YOU WANT IS
NOTHING NO MATTER HOW HARD YOU FOUGHT.
WHAT GOD HAS IN STORE FOR YOU
WILL EXCEED WHATEVER YOU THOUGHT!

EXPECT THE UNEXPECTED

GOD WILL USE ANYONE
TO CARRY OUT HIS WILL.
HE IS IN CONTROL OF ALL THINGS
AND HIS ULTIMATE POWER IS FOR REAL.

JUST BECAUSE SOMEONE LOOKS UNLIKELY
THEY ARE PRECIOUS IN HIS SIGHT.
GOD CHOOSES THE CHOSEN FOR
THE JOB HE KNOWS THEY'RE RIGHT.

GOD USES THE UNSUSPECTED BROKEN
VESSEL SO HE WILL GET THE GLORY.
WHEN IT'S ALL SAID AND DONE
IT'S TRULY A MIRACULOUS STORY.

GOD TOOK THE PROFESSION FORNICATOR
WASHED HIM UP AS WHITE AS SNOW.
NOW HE TEACHES OTHERS
TO TITHES AND TO SEED SOW.

GOD TOOK THE ROLLING STONE OF A
FATHER FILLED HIM WITH THE HOLY GHOST.
THEN PUT HIM IN THE MALE CHORUS
BECAUSE THAT'S WHERE HE WAS NEEDED THE MOST.

GOD DELIVERED THE CLUB HOPPING YOUNGSTER
AND MADE HER A LEADER ON THE PRAISE DANCE TEAM.
SHE DANCED SO SPLENDED AND GRACEFUL
SHE DAZZLED LIKE A BRIGHT SUNBEAM.

GOD TURNED THE STREET SMART HARLOT
INTO A PROPHET FOR THE DIVINE.
CAUSE THAT IS JUST AS AMAZING
AS TURNING WATER INTO WINE.

NOW IF JESUS CAN RAISE
LAZARUS BACK FROM THE DEAD.
AND CAST OUT LEGIONS OF DEMONS
AS THE BIBLE CLEARLY SAID.

HE CAN DIG WAY DOWN MAKE
YOUR LIFE NOW WHOLE.
HE CAN SHINE YOU UP COMPLETELY
YOU'LL BE WORTH YOUR WEIGHT IN GOLD.

EXPECT GOD TO DO THE UNEXPECTED
JUST SIT BACK, WATCH, AND SEE.
THEY'LL BE TRANSFORMED BEFORE YOUR
EYES AND ALL THEIR SINS WILL FLEE.

GOD CLEANED UP THE ALCOHOLIC TOUCHED
HIS HEART AND NOW HE PREACHES.
GOD TURNED AROUND THE ADULTERER EQUIPPED
HER WITH THE WORD NOW SUNDAY
SCHOOL SHE TEACHES.

GOD TOOK THE UNWED MOTHER TOUCHED
HER HANDS TO HEAL THE WEAK.
THERE IS NOTHING GOD CAN'T DO
FOR HE MADE THE DONKEY SPEAK.

JUST AS GOD OPENED THE RED SEA
FOR MOSES AND THE OTHERS TO CROSS.
GOD DELIVERED THE LESBIAN WOMAN
TO MAKE CERTAIN HER SOUL WON'T BE LOST.

GOD SET FREE THE HOMOSEXUAL MAN
GAVE HIM A SONG TO LEAD IN THE CHOIR.
THE REQUIREMENTS FOR THIS POSITION
DID NOT CARE WHAT HE HAD DONE PRIOR.

GOD TOOK THE DRUG DEALER GAVE HIM A
MINISTRY TO REACH THE PEOPLE ON THE STREET.
HE TOOK ONE WHO WAS DEEP IN IDOLATRY
AND IN THE PULPIT IS WHERE SHE TOOK A SEAT.

GOD LOOSED THE CRACK ADDICT AND
HE BECAME A LEADER OF PRAISE.
HE WAS SO GRATEFUL HE GAVE GOD
THE GLORY ALL THE REST OF HIS DAYS.

GOD TOOK THE THIEF CAST OUT THAT
DEMON AND MADE HIM A CHURCH DOORKEEPER.
FOR WHAT THE LORD HAD DONE FOR HIM
MADE HIM LOVE AND ADORE GOD MUCH DEEPER.

IT DOES NOT MATTER THE POSITION
YOU HOLD OR ANY OTHERS WAY BACK.
GOD WILL GIVE YOU ALL YOU NEED
AND FILL YOU WITH ALL YOU LACK.

GOD USES THE FOOLISH ACCORDING TO
THE STANDARDS OF MERE MAN.
GOD IS ALMIGHTY AND POWERFUL HE HOLDS
THE WHOLE WORLD IN THE PALM OF HIS HAND.

SO DON'T THINK YOU CAN'T BE USED
BECAUSE OF WHAT YOU DID BEFORE.
YOU CAN STILL BE RICH TODAY
ALTHOUGH YOU WERE BORN POOR.

DON'T LET WHAT YOU USED TO DO STOP
YOU FROM ACHIEVING YOUR VERY BEST.
LEARN FROM PAST MISTAKES TO BE
CERTAIN YOU PASS THE NEXT TEST.

JESUS TOOK 2 FISH AND 5 LOAVES OF
BREAD TO FEED A HUNGRY CREW.
THIS IS NOTHING COMPARED TO WHAT
THE LORD WILL DO FOR ME AND YOU.

EXPECT GOD TO DO THE UNEXPECTED
SIT BACK, WATCH, AND SEE.
YOU'LL BE TRANSFORMED BEFORE YOUR
EYES AND ALL YOUR SINS WILL FLEE.

YOU STRONG BLACK WOMAN, YOU

THOUGH YOU HAVE ENDURED
GREAT LOSS IN THIS LIFE.
YES, YOU HAVE CERTAINLY
HAD YOUR SHARE OF STRIFE.

YOU STILL STOOD TALL WITH
YOUR HEAD HELD SO HIGH.
I WANT TO BE JUST LIKE
YOU AND THAT IS NO LIE.

YOU STRONG, BLACK WOMAN, YOU!

THOUGH MANY YEARS HAVE PASSED
YOU HAVEN'T LOST YOUR STRUT.
YOU'RE AS TOUGH AS DIAMONDS
HARD GLASS YOU CAN CUT.

YOU'VE BEEN THROUGH THE STORM
YOU'VE BEEN THOUGH THE RAIN.
YOU'VE BEEN THROUGH MUCH YET YOU
SEEM UNTOUCHED BY THE PAIN.

YOU STRONG, BLACK WOMAN, YOU!

YOU'VE BEEN THROUGH THE FIRE
AND SEEN YOUR SKY TURN GRAY.
YET YOU HELD ON
TO SEE A BRIGHTER DAY.

I APPLAUD YOU DEAR LADY
YOU'VE PROVED WHO IS WHO.
A RARE JEWEL AND PRICELESS INSPITE
OF WHAT YOU'VE BEEN THROUGH.

YOU STRONG, BLACK WOMAN, YOU!

IN THE MIDST OF IT ALL
STILL FOCUSED YOU STOOD.
YOU WALKED RIGHT ON THROUGH
LIKE I KNEW YOU COULD.

GOD BLESS YOU FOR YOUR
STRENGTH AND ALSO YOUR GRACE.
IN THE LAMB'S BOOK OF LIFE
THIS WON'T BE ERASED.

YOU STRONG, BLACK WOMAN, YOU

DEDICATED TO

MY AUNT "MOMMA HAZEL"
HAZEL WINGATE LYMAN

TOUCH NOT MY ANOINTED

TOUCH NOT MY ANOINTED
DO MY PROPHET NO HARM.
HONOR THIS REQUEST SO
GOD YOU WON'T ALARM.
DO YOU KNOW WHO IS ANOINTED
BY JUST LOOKING AT THEIR FACE.
TO BE ON THE SAFE SIDE KEEP YOUR MOUTH
OFF OTHERS IN THE FIRST DOGGONE PLACE.

NO WEAPON FORMED AGAINST ME SHALL PROSPER
SO IT WON'T WORK ANYWAY.
IF SOMEHOW I OFFEND YOU, DON'T
YOU KNOW YOU'RE SUPPOSE TO PRAY.
THE NEGATIVE ENERGY YOU SEND OUT
WILL TURN BACK TO YOU, YOU KNOW.
REMEMBER YOU ALWAYS REAP FAR GREATER
THAN YOU COULD POSSIBLY SOW.

THE POSITIVE ENERGY IS JUST THE SAME
YOU SEND OUT WHAT YOU GET BACK.
AND IF YOU CAN'T SAY SOMETHING GOOD
DON'T INSTEAD LAUNCH AN ATTACK.
DO UNTO OTHERS AS YOU WOULD
HAVE THEM DO UNTO YOU.
IF YOU LET YOUR SPIRIT LEAD
YOU WON'T FIND THIS HARD TO DO.

FLESH IS WHAT TRIGGERS YOU TO
DO WHAT YOU KNOW IS WRONG.
THE DEVIL MADE ME DO IT IS
A SORRY, SAD OLD SONG.
WATCH WHAT YOU LET COME OUT
OF THAT VERY MOUTH OF YOURS.
AS SLOW TO SPEAK IS ONE OF
ALL OUR SPIRITUAL CHORES.

ONE SHOULD TEST THE MOTIVE OF
ONLY HIS VERY OWN ACTIONS.
I PRAY WHAT YOU FIND IS HONORABLE
AND IN NO WAY AN INFRACTION.
IF YOU TEST YOURSELF YOU'LL HAVE
NO PROBLEM DOING WHAT IS RIGHT.
THIS WILL KEEP YOU IN LINE SO YOUR
OWN TONGUE YOU WON'T HAVE TO BITE!

TOUCH NOT MY ANOINTED
DO MY PROPHETS NO PAIN.
SO THEY'LL BE NO PROBLEMS AND GOD'S
WRATH WILL NOT BE ORDAINED!

YOUR BABY'S DADDY

IF YOU DON'T KNOW WHO YOUR
BABY'S DADDY IS JUST SAY SO.

IT WOULD SOLVE A LOT OF PROBLEMS,
A LOT OF GRIEF AND WOE.

DON'T YOU KNOW THE
TRUTH SHALL MAKE YOU FREE.

LET HIM KNOW HE IS A CANDIDATE
AND AFTER THE BIRTH THE TEST WILL SEE.

DON'T TELL HIM, HE IS THE ONLY ONE
IF YOU KNOW HE'S REALLY NOT.

BE HONEST WITH YOURSELF AND HIM,
DON'T JUST FILL THE SLOT.

THAT WAY YOUR CHILD WON'T HAVE TO GO
THOUGH THE REVOLVING DADDY DOOR.

BECAUSE YOU WERE TRUTHFUL FROM
THE START AND GOT RIGHT TO THE CORE.

YES, IT IS A HARD PILL TO SWALLOW BUT
YOU'VE GOT TO DO WHAT'S RIGHT.

IT WILL PAY OFF IN THE END AND
SAVE YOU FROM AN AWFUL FRIGHT.

I WONDER HOW MANY DADDIES
ARE REALLY NOT DADDIES AT ALL.

THEY SIMPLY GOT TRAPPED IN THE LIAR'S
NET AND SET UP FOR THE FALL.

TURN OUT TO BE FOR GOOD

IF YOU DIG A DITCH FOR SOMEONE, YOU
DON'T REALLY HAVE TO DIG TWO.

BECAUSE NO MATTER HOW MANY YOU DIG
THEY WILL ONLY BE FOR YOU.

REVENGE IS NOT YOURS FROM
EITHER ANGLE YOU LOOK.

REGARDLESS OF WHAT WAS DONE OR
WHATEVER FROM YOU WAS TOOK.

EVERYTHING THAT'S GIVEN TO YOU
MAY ONLY BE THERE FOR A SEASON.

TO BUILD YOUR CHARACTER OR INCREASE
YOUR FAITH, I TELL YOU THIS FOR THAT REASON.

JUST LET GOD HANDLE HIS BUSINESS,
I KNOW, YOU KNOW HE COULD.

CAUSE SOMETIMES THINGS WE THINK
ARE BAD TURN OUT TO BE FOR GOOD.

JUST MY OPINION

I WOULD RATHER BE IN PHYSICAL PAIN
THAN HURT TO MY MENTAL STATE

BECAUSE EFFECT OF THE MENTAL
MAY NOT SURFACE UNTIL ITS TOO LATE.

A BURSTED LIP, A BLACKEN EYE
SURELY IN TIME WILL HEAL.

MENTAL PAIN MAY LIE DORMANT THEN
MOVE IN EQUIPPED TO KILL.

A PAIN MEDICINE OR JUST SOME REST
FOR THE BODY MAY BE JUST THE THING.

BUT FOR MENTAL AILMENTS IT MAY
TAKE ROOT AND START TO CLING.

YOU'LL NEVER KNOW WHAT HAPPENED
WHEN IT UP AND STARTS TO GROW.

IT WILL STRESS YOU OUT COMPLETELY,
THEN IT WILL TIE YOU IN A BOW.

LIKE THE SMELL OF GARBAGE
IT BEGINS TO HAVE A STENCH.

IT WILL CREEP INTO YOU CONSCIENCE
AND TAKE YOU LIFE WITHIN AN INCH.

WE THINK ONLY TIME WILL
HEAL EMOTIONAL BUMPS AND STRAINS.

BUT SOMETIMES THAT IS AS BAD AS
PUTTING A BANDAGE ON SEVERE CHEST PAINS.

PHYSICAL PAIN IS AWFUL TO ME,
MENTAL PAIN EXCEEDS THE REST.

SEEK PROFESSIONAL HELP WITH EITHER
TO HELP YOU GET RID OF THIS PEST.

TIME BOMB

LIVING WITH A TIME BOMB READY
TO GO OFF AT ANYTIME.

THE SLIGHTEST FLINCH CAN MAKE IT
EXPLODE AT THE DROP OF A DIME.

WHO WANTS TO LIVE ON EGGSHELLS
AFRAID TO MAKE A MOVE.

NOT KNOWING WHAT WILL HAPPEN
IF THE OTHER ONE DISAPPROVES.

UNABLE TO BE YOURSELF OR
DARE TO DREAM A BIT.

WITHOUT THE MISERY OF WONDERING
IF SOMEONE WILL HAVE A FIT.

HOW LONG CAN YOU GO ON LIKE THIS,
BEFORE IT ALL GETS RATHER OLD.

ANYTHING THAT'S GOING BAD IN
TIME WILL SURELY GROW MOLD.

STOP THE TIME BOMB IN ITS TRACKS
AND DON'T LET IT BULLY YOU AROUND.

YOU MUST LOOK IT DEAD IN THE EYES
AND FIGHT IT POUND FOR POUND.

DON'T GET ME WRONG THIS IS NO PHYSICAL FIGHT,
REBUKE IT, IT MUST SUBMIT.

IF YOU DO IT IN JESUS' NAME, IT
HAS NO CHOICE BUT TO QUIT.

WE HAVE THE POWER, YES INDEED
TO DECLARE THE SPIRIT TO FLEE.

WE JUST NEED TO TAKE A STAND AND
WE WILL SURELY SEE.

FLOW OF BLESSINGS

THERE ARE BLESSINGS FALLING FROM
HEAVEN
BUT YOU'VE GOT TO BE LINED UP TO
RECEIVE.

BLESSINGS IN ABUNDANCE AVAILABLE
TO ALL THAT TRULY BELIEVE.

JUST LIKE WHEN YOU TAKE A SHOWER TO
GET WET YOU MUST STAND UNDER.
.
OR AN UMBRELLA YOU PUT OVER YOUR
HEAD WHEN IT RAINS AND THUNDERS.

YOU MUST GET LINED UP FOR THESE
BLESSINGS WITH YOUR ARMS OPEN WIDE.

AND IF YOU'RE RIGHT UNDERNEATH THEM
IN YOUR ARMS THESE BLESSINGS WITH SLIDE.

LIFE

DON'T TRY TO ANALYZE LIFE BECAUSE
YOU CAN'T SEE THE FULL PICTURE.
A PROSPEROUS LIFE MAY NOT MAKE
YOUR WALLET MILLIONS RICHER.

YOU MAY OR MAY NOT LIVE TO BE 102
MAKE SURE YOU RECEIVE ALL THAT YOU ARE DUE.
DON'T CHEAT YOUSELF TIME AND TIME AGAIN
I WANT YOU TO SUCCEED IN LIFE MY DEAR FRIEND.

IT'S NOT THE QUANITY BUT ITS
THE QUALITY OF LIFE THAT'S BEST.
LEARN ALL YOUR LIFE'S LESSONS
AND PASS ALL YOUR LIFE'S TESTS.

FROM THE TIME YOU WERE BORN YOU
HAVE A SET NUMBER OF HOURS GOD KNOWS.
YOUR ACTUAL MOMENT OF CONCEPTION
IN HIS HANDS HE HOLDS ALL POWERS.

JUST AS GOD NOWS THE SPECIFIC
NUMBER OF HAIRS ON YOUR HEAD.
HE EVEN KNOWS AT YOUR BIRTH
EXACTLY WHO YOU WILL WED.

DURING A LIFETIME ONE TOUCHES
SO MANY DIFFERENT PATHS.
SOME MOMENT ARE DEEPLY SADDEN
AND OTHERS ARE FULL OF MANY LAUGHS.

EACH DIFFERENT ACT OPENS A DOOR
TO WHERE YOU'VE NEVER BEEN.
LIVE EVERYDAY TO THE FULLEST CAUSE
YOU DON'T KNOW WHERE IT WILL END.

THE LAST TIME YOU SEE A PERSON YOU
DON'T KNOW THAT'S THE LAST SCENE.
SO DON'T SAY OR DO ANYTHING YOU
KNOW YOU REALLY DON'T MEAN.

IN EVERYTHING YOU DO GIVE GLORY
AND GOD'S PRAISES ALWAYS SING.
BECAUSE TO BE ABSENT FROM THE BODY
IS TO BE PRESENT WITH THE KING.

SOULMATE

HAVE YOU EVER MET THAT SOMEONE WHOM
IT SEEMS YOU CAN'T LIVE WITHOUT?
THAT SOMEONE WHO YOU KNOW IS YOUR TRUE
SOULMATE WITHOUT ANY KIND OF A DOUBT.
THAT PERSON THAT CAN SPEAK THE VERY SAME
WORDS YOU HAVE ONLY IN YOUR MIND.
THE ONE WHO CAN FINISH YOUR
SENTENCES EACH AND EVERY SINGLE TIME.

THAT PERSON WHO MAKES YOUR HEART SKIP
A BEAT WHENEVER THEY ARE NEAR.
THE ONE YOU LOVE IN YOUR HEART
EVER SO PRECIOUS AND OH YES SO CLEAR.
YOU DON'T FIND LOVE LIKE THIS
EVERYDAY NOT EVEN EVERY WEEK.
IT DOES NOT COME OFTEN NO
MATTER HOW FREQUENTLY YOU SEEK.

LOVE SO INNOCENT
SO PURE AND SO REAL.
SO PASSIONATE IS MAKES
YOUR ENTIRE EXISTENCE FEEL.
TO FINALLY MEET THE
LOVE OF YOUR LIFE.
IT'S SO PROFOUND
IT CUTS LIKE A KNIFE.

IT'S JUST OVERWHELMING
YOU KNOW FROM THE START.
THAT THIS IS THE ONE WHOM
YOU SHARE THE SAME HEART.
YOU CAME INTO MY LIFE LIKE
A THIEF IN THE NIGHT.
I LOVED YOU SO INSTANTLY
IT WAS QUITE A FRIGHT.

IT'S FUNNY, IT'S NOT JUST
A PHYSICAL THING.
YOU UPLIFT MY SPIRIT
AND NOW IT HAS WINGS.
MY LOVE CUP HAS SOMEHOW
COMPLETELY OVERFLOWED.
MY HEART AND MY BREATH HAS
SOMEWHAT NOW SLOWED.

FOR THE AFFECTIONS OF MY
HEART HE KNOWS HE HAS FIRST DIBS
YES, I AM THE WOMAN
WHO WAS MADE FROM HIS OWN RIB.
I DON'T KNOW WHAT'S TO COME
I ONLY KNOW WHAT'S BEEN.
BUT SOMEHOW MY HEART KNOWS I'LL
NEVER LOVE THIS WAY AGAIN.

MOMMA'S BABY PAPA'S MAYBE

SHE WAS THIRTEEN, PREGNANT,
AND VERY MUCH AFRAID.
SHE THOUGHT HER LIFE WAS OVER
BECAUSE OF THE MESS SHE'D MADE.

WHY WAS SHE THE ONLY ONE TO SUFFER,
TO HURT, AND TO TAKE THE BLAME?
SHE DIDN'T GET THIS WAY ALONE
SHOULDN'T HE BE FEELING THE SAME.

NO, ALL ALONE SHE STOOD BUT
HE NEVER EVEN LOOKED BACK.
DID'NT KNOW IF HE WAS THE
FATHER, HE COULDN'T BE EXACT.

THE OLD SAYING FITS THIS ON THE
HEAD MOMA'S BABY PAPA'S MAYBE.
BUT SHOULDN'T PAPA STICK
AROUND EVEN IF ONLY TO SEE?

IF HE IS NOT YOUR CHILD GO ON, NO
LOSS CAUSE YOU ARE NOT THE BLAME.
BUT IF HE IS YOUR BLOOD, DON'T YOU
WANT HIM TO HAVE YOUR NAME?

IT'S JUST NOT FAIR TO LEAVE THIS
GIRL ALONE TO HOLD THE BAG.
DON'T MAKE YOUR COULD BE CHILD
SUFFER THIS IS IN NO WAY A GAG.

IF YOU WALK AWAY WITHOUT KNOWING
I PROMISE YOU WILL NOT FORGET.
YOU'LL SPEND YOUR TIME IN WHAT IF
LAND AND THIS I'M WILLING TO BET.

IT MAY TAKE MONTHS OF PATIENCE
BUT SOON YOU'LL SURELY KNOW.
YOUR CONSCIENCE WILL NOT BOTHER
YOU EITHER WAY IT GO.

MAMA'S BABY PAPA'S MAYBE
IS WHAT FOLKS USED TO SAY.
BE RESPONSIBLE DO YOUR PART SO
REGRET YOU WON'T FACE ONE DAY.

MY JOURNEY

THROUGH ALL THE HEARTACHES AND PAIN
THROUGH ALL THE STORM AND THE RAIN
I WOULDN'T GIVE OR TAKE NOTHING FOR MY JOURNEY.

FOR MY FAILURES AND HARD TRIALS
FOR ALL THE KNOCKS AND ALL THE LONG MILES
I WOULDN'T GIVE OR TAKE NOTHING FOR MY JOURNEY.

THOUGH I'VE LOST MANY LOVED ONES ALONG THE WAY
ALL OF THEM I SHALL SEE AGAIN ONE FINE DAY.
I WOULDN'T GIVE OR TAKE NOTHING FOR MY JOURNEY.

MY JOURNEY MAKES ME WHO I AM
AND THIS IS HOW IS FELT
I SURELY WOULDN'T WANT TO REACH MY
DESTINY WITHOUT THIS EXPERIENCE UNDER MY BELT.
SO AGAIN I SAY, I WOULDN'T GIVE OR
TAKE NOTHING FOR MY JOURNEY.

THE SPIRIT

SOME SAY THE FUTURE IS UNCERTAIN AND
THIS MAKES THEM AFRAID OF THE UNKNOWN.
SOME SEE THE FUTURE BEFORE IT HAPPENS
BECAUSE IN THEIR DREAMS THEY ARE SHOWN.

THE ABILITY TO DO THIS IS ONE
OF GOD'S MOST PRECIOUS GIFTS.
TO GET TO THE TRUE MEANING THROUGH
THE DREAM YOU MUST CAREFULLY SIFT.

SORTING EVERY DETAIL FROM
EVERY DIFFERENT ANGLE.
YOU WILL SEE WHAT IS TO COME
IN THE DREAM YOU WILL UNMANGLE.

THE POURING OUT OF GOD'S SPIRIT
HAS CAUSED THIS EVENT TO OCCUR.
THE VESSEL MUST BE SOLD OUT, WILLING,
AND COME TO GOD JUST AS YOU WERE.

DON'T FORGET ABOUT THE VISIONS
THAT MEN WILL HONESTLY SEE.
AND THE UTTERANCE OF DIFFERENT
TONGUES TO EDITIFY ONLY THEE.

MEN AND WOMEN WILL SURELY PROPHESY WHEN
I POUR OUT MY SPIRIT IN THOSE DAYS.
DREAM, DREAMS AND SEE VISIONS IS
WHAT THE BIBLE CLEARLY SAYS.

GOD WILL SHOW WONDERS IN HEAVEN
AND SIGNS ON THE EARTH BELOW.
WE SEE THIS EVERYDAY AS
WE TRAVEL TO AND FRO.

BEFORE THING SPRING INTO EXISTENCE
GOD MAY SHOW IT TO YOU PRIOR.
THIS IS A GIFT SENT FROM THE
LORD TO HELP YOU TO INSPIRE.

DON'T BE AFRAID OF THE FUTURE FOR
YESTERDAY'S TOMMORROW IS TODAY.
JUST PUT YOUR TRUST IN JESUS
HE WILL HELP YOU EVERY STEP OF THE WAY.

ONE MUST LEAD THE WAY

FOR CENTRIES WHETHER IT'S MARRIAGE,
FRIENDSHIP, OR BROTHERHOOD
ONE MUST LEAD THE WAY.
ONE WILL GO ON TO ETERNITY THE
OTHER IS LEFT HERE FOR A WHILE TO STAY.
ONE MUST LEAD THE WAY THE
OTHER ONE WILL HAVE TO FOLLOW.
ONE WILL BITE THE DUST THE
OTHER TEARS WILL SWALLOW.

NO MATTER HOW YOU PUT IT
ONE MUST DEFINITELY GO FIRST.
TO LEAVE THE OTHER HERE ALONE
AND FEELING THEIR HEART HAS BURST.
ONE MUST GO FIRST MY
GRANDFATHER USED TO SAY.
SHORTLY, AFTER HE LEFT THIS WORLD
AND HIS GRAVE IS WHERE HIS BODY LAY.

IT'S FUNNY HOW WE NEVER THINK
OF BEING LEFT BEHIND.
I DON'T KNOW WHICH IS WORST GOING
ON OR BEING THE ONE IN LINE.
NO ONE REALLY THINKS ABOUT,
"UNTIL DEATH DO WE PART."
WE THINK THIS WILL NEVER HAPPEN
AND WE'LL NEVER HAVE THIS BROKEN HEART.

ALL THESE RELATIONSHIPS LAST FOREVER
EVEN WHEN ONE PASSES ON.
MEMORIES CONTINUE TO LIVE EVEN
WHEN ONE PARTNER'S GONE.
AS LONG AS THE ONE THAT LEFT
STILL CHERISHES THE PAST.
THIS RELATIONSHIP DOESN'T DIE
AND WILL CONTINUE TO LAST.

I HAVE BEEN THE ONE THAT'S LEFT ONE DAY
I'LL BE THE ONE WHO LEAVES.
LIFE IS A WOVEN CYCLE OF UPS AND
DOWNS I REALLY DO BELIEVE.
I DON'T KNOW WHICH I'D
RATHER BE BUT BOTH I KNOW, I WILL.
AS LONG AS I HAVE SOME RELATIONSHIPS
I KNOW THAT LOVE IS REAL.

IN LOVING MEMORY OF MY GRANDDADDIES

SHIRLEY WINGATE, SR.
PENSACOLA, FL

PERRY RICHARD, SR.
APALACHICOLA, FL

ALPHA AND OMEGA

WHO KNOWS BETWEEN US ALL WHO
WILL BE THE ONE TO GO HOME FIRST.
LOOK AT THIS CAREFULLY, TO GO OR STAY
WHICH WOULD BE THE VERY WORST?

THE ALPHA GOES TO LEAD THE WAY
THE OTHERS TOO MUST CROSS.
BUT OMEGA WILL BEFORE THE END
EXPERIENCE SUCH GREAT LOSS.

ALPHA WILL CROSS TO THE
NEXT LIFE ONLY TO BE REBORN.
OMEGA WILL BE LEFT BEHIND TIME
AFTER TIME TO GRIEVE AND MOURN.

GREAT COURAGE IS NEEDED TO LEAVE
THIS WORLD AND BE THE PIONEER.
LONG SUFFERING IS WHAT COMES
TO MIND FOR THE ONE LEFT IN THE REAR.

CAN YOU IMAGINE SEEING ALL YOU
LOVE FROM THEIR BODY GONE?
AND YOU LEFT HERE TO CARRY ON
IN THE DARKNESS WITH NO DAWN.

WHEN YOUR TIME COMES THE LIGHT IS
THERE TO MARK YOUR JOURNEY'S PATH.
IF NOT DESTRUCTION COMES
THEN WILL COME THE WRATH.

THE DATE YOU'RE BORN AND THE DATE
YOU DIE IS ALREADY MADE IN TIME.
YOU CAN NOT RESCHEDULE OR
PUT IT OFF BECAUSE IT'S PREDESTINED.

ONE THING THAT IS FOR SURE
WE ALL MUST WALK THE FINAL LAP.
OUR DATE WITH DEATH HAS BEEN
ARRANGED AND IS NOT A MISHAP.

GOD BLESS US ALL NO MATTER
WHAT OUR STATUS IS IN LINE.
FOR TO BE ABSENT FROM THE BODY
IS TO BE PRESENT WITH THE DIVINE.

IN LOVING MEMORY OF MY GREAT GRANDPARENTS

REV. ESAU AND MRS. NORA LONDON
PENSACOLA, FL

SELF PITY

HAVE YOU EVER BEEN SO SAD
YOU COULDN'T FEEL YOUR SOUL.
SO NUMB FROM EMOTIONS IT SEEMS
RELIEF WILL NEVER BE UNFOLD.

HOW DEEP ROOTED IS THE FEELINGS
TO PULL IT UP WILL TAKE YOUR ALL.
WHETHER ITS GRIEF OR SORROW IT
HAS MADE YOU SLUMP AND FALL.

BUT YOU DON'T HAVE TO STAY THERE
TO WALLOW IN THE PAIN.
YOU REALLY DON'T HAVE TO BE
MISERABLE OR DRIVE YOURSELF INSANE.

JUST GIVE YOUR BURDENS TO JESUS
THEN WATCH HIM WORK ON YOUR BEHALF.
HE WILL PICK YOU UP, TURN YOU AROUND,
THEN SET YOU BACK ON THE RIGHT PATH.

SATAN USES EMOTIONS TO TAKE
US OFF OF OUR GIVEN COURSE.
I GUESS HE HAS FORGOTTEN OUR
POWER COMES FROM AN UNLIMITED SOURCE.

GOD WILL NEVER EVER FORSAKE US,
WE TURN AWAY FROM HIM.
THEN WE LIE IN OUR OWN SELF PITY
AND LET OUR LIGHTS GROW DIM.

IF YOU SLIP DON'T SIDE
IS WHAT FOLKS USED TO SAY.
PICK YOURSELF UP, DUST YOURSELF OFF
GOD WILL SURELY MAKE A WAY.

IF YOU EVER BECOME SO SAD
YOU CAN NOT FEEL YOUR SOUL,
GO TO JESUS FOR REFUGE HE'LL
SHELTER YOU FROM THE COLD.

ALMOST ABORTED

FROM THE EYES OF A CHILD
THAT WAS ALMOST ABORTED.
IF MY GRANNY HADN'T THREATENED MY MOM
I WOULD HAVE BEEN DISTORTED.

SUCKED OUT BY A VACUUM
PIECE BY PIECE.
I NEVER WOULD HAVE BEEN BORN
TO SAY THE VERY LEAST.

I NEVER WOULD HAVE HAD THE CHANCE
TO HAVE MY GREAT CHILDHOOD.
I NEVER WOULD HAVE MADE MY MOMA
PROUD THE WAY I KNEW I WOULD.

MY FIRST STEP, MY FIRST WORD
MY FIRST FULL NIGHT OF SLEEP.
NEVER WOULD HAVE BEEN SACRED
IN MY BABY BOOK TO KEEP.

I WOULD HAVE ONLY BEEN A BAD MEMORY
OR AN EXPERIENCE YOU TRIED TO FORGET.
EVERY TIME YOU LOOKED IN THE
MIRROR MY DEMISE YOU WOULD REGRET.

WE ARE SUCH A VERY CLOSE FAMILY,
MOMMA, GRANDMOMMA, AND ME.
NO ONE EVER WOULD HAVE
THOUGHT I ALMOST DIDN'T BE.

MOM I KNOW THAT YOU WERE YOUNG
AND DIDN'T KNOW JUST WHAT TO DO.
THE MERE THOUGHT OF BEING A MOTHER
WAS TO YOU ALSO BRAND NEW.

I GUESS THAT'S WHY I'M SPECIAL
AND I KNOW I'M IN GOD'S PLAN.
I KNOW I'M SUPPOSED TO BE HERE
AND ON ME GOD'S GOT HIS HAND.

I'M GLAD MY GRANDMOMMA SPOKE UP FOR ME
AND MY MOM TOOK HEED AS WELL.
I THANK THEM BOTH EVERYDAY ALTHOUGH
I DON'T GO INTO DETAILS.

MAKE ME CAREFUL

LORD MAKE ME CAREFUL NOT TO LET MY
HAPPINESS HURT ANYONE ALONG THE WAY.
FOR I WANT TO BE POSITIVE, SO TEACH
ME TO WATCH THE WORDS I SAY.

DON'T ALLOW ME TO GET HIGH AND
MIGHTY OR LET ME ACT SO GRAND.
PLEASE BUILD ME UP TO HANDLE THIS
HAPPINESS TO NOT INTERFERE WITH YOUR PLAN.

FOR IT IS NOT ALL ABOUT ME AND
I AM GRATEFUL TO BASK IN YOUR PLEASURE.
YOU HAVE BEEN MIGHTY GOOD TO ME
ALL YOUR GOODNESS I CAN'T EVEN MEASURE.

INCREASE MY CONCERNS FOR OTHERS
AS IN YOUR SIGHT I WANT TO DO WHAT'S PROPER.
IN MY HEART I WANT TO BE LIKE YOU
I WANT TO BE GOLD NOT COPPER.

QUICKEN MY SPIRIT TO BE AWARE OF OTHERS
SO THEIR SPIRIT WILL NOT BE DEPLETED.
BECAUSE YOU SAID TO TREAT OTHERS THE
WAY THAT WE WOULD LIKE TO BE TREATED.

GUIDE MY TONGUE AND ACTIONS TO ENSURE
THE HEARTS OF OTHERS I DON'T CRUSH.
BECAUSE MY INTENTIONS ARE TO UPLIFT
OTHERS NOT TO CAUSE SADNESS OR FLUSH.

DELIVERED

WE ALL HAVE NEEDED TO BE DELIVERED
FROM SOMETHING OR ANOTHER.

NO ONE IS EXEMPT NOT EVEN
YOUR DEAR SWEET MOTHER.

SIN IS A SIN IS A SIN FROM
DAY START TO DAY DONE.

NO ONE IS PERFECT
NO NOT EVEN ONE.

THERE IS NO SIN THAT IS
JUSTIFIED BEFORE ANOTHER.

SO DON'T TRY TO CONVINCE ANYONE
YOUR SIN IS BETTER THAN YOUR BROTHER'S.

THE BIBLE SIMPLY TELL US
JUDGE NOT LEST YE BE JUDGED.

THE SIN YOU THOUGHT WAS JUST A
DOT MAY ACTUALLY BE A LARGE SMUDGE.

ALL SIN CAN BE FORGIVEN
AS EASILY AS THE NEXT.

CONFESS YOUR SINS TO GOD THE
PROCEDURE IS NEVER COMPLEX.

HELP IS ON THE WAY

TO THINK THAT SUICIDE IS THE ANSWER
IS STRAIGHT FROM THE PIT OF HELL.

SATAN WANTS YOU BOUND AND BROKEN
SO YOUR DEMISE WILL BE A HIDEOUS TALE.

HOW COULD YOU THINK THAT TAKING
YOUR LIFE IS GOD'S MOST PERFECT WILL?

IT IS A DEVIOUS PLOY SO YOUR TRUE
IDENTITY WILL NEVER BE REVEALED.

SOMEONE IS COUNTING ON YOU
TO MAKE SURE THEY'RE NEEDS ARE MET.

SOMEONE NEEDS YOUR ENCOURAGEMENT
SO THEY WON'T HAVE TO FRET.

WHAT WOULD THEY DO IF YOU'RE
NOT HERE TO SAVE THEM FROM THEMSELVES.

GOD SENT HIS SON TO PAY YOUR COST
CAUSE YOU ARE WORTH GREAT WEALTH.

IF YOU WOULD TAKE YOUR LIFE TODAY
YOU WILL NEVER SEE TOMORROW.

YOU WILL LEAVE YOUR FRIENDS AND
FAMILY HERE TO FACE THE SADDEST SORROW.

DON'T YOU KNOW YOUR BREAK
THROUGH IS NOT THAT FAR AWAY.

DON'T GIVE UP, CAUSE DON'T YOU
KNOW GOD HAS THE FINAL SAY.

YOU NEVER WOULD HAVE BEEN HERE IF YOU
WERE NOT SUPPOSED TO HELP ALONG THE WAY

HE WILL NEVER GIVE YOU MORE
THAN YOUR SHARE THE ANSWER IS TO PRAY.

ASK GOD TO HELP YOU TO ENDURE
THE PAIN CAN ONLY LAST A SEASON.

HOLD ON HELP IS ON THE WAY I
TELL YOU THIS FOR THAT REASON.

MY APOLOGY

IN MY LIFE I'VE DONE SOMETHINGS
THAT HURT OTHERS IN MY PATH.

BELIEVE ME BECAUSE OF MY CARELESSNESS,
I HAVE REAPED THE MASTER'S WRATH.

THE WORD SAYS ANYONE WHO DOES
WRONG WILL CERTAINLY BE REPAID.

I HAVEN'T ASKED FOR EXEMPTION
BUT FORGIVENESS IS WHAT I PRAYED.

IT ALSO SAYS ONE WHO PLEASES HIS SINFUL
NATURE FROM THE SAME HE WILL REAP.

IN THE POOL OF SINFULNESS
I SANK IN FAR TOO DEEP.

REPAYMENT IS MY PENALTY
AND I DESERVE JUST THAT.

I FACED THIS SENTENCE LIKE A MAN
AND CONVICTION IS WHERE I SAT.

IF ONLY I WOULD HAVE RESPONDED
IN A DIFFERENT WAY.

I WOULD NOT HAVE TO FEEL THIS GUILT
AND HAVE TO REPENT THIS DAY.

I HAVE CONFESSED MY SINS TO
THE ALMIGHTY AND POWERFUL MISTER.

DEEP INSIDE I FEEL THE URGE TO
DO THE SAME TO MY SISTER.

I SAY THIS TO YOU THE HUMBLEST WAY
THAT I HONESTLY KNOW HOW.

I WAS NOT THINKING AT THE
TIME BUT I AM THINKING NOW.

HOW COULD I HURT YOU LIKE THIS
BY COMMITTING THIS UNSPEAKABLE DEED.

I HURT YOU UNDESERVINGLY
BECAUSE OF MY OWN SELFISH NEED.

I HAVE FELT YOUR EXACT SAME PAIN BEFORE
ALTHOUGH IT WAS WAY BACK WHEN.

THE NERVE OF ME TO INFLICT SUCH HURT
WHEN IN YOUR SHOES BEFORE I'VE BEEN.

IT WAS AN OVERWHELMING, COMPELLING
FORCE THAT GOT ME INTO THIS MESS.

IF I HAD BEEN STRONGER I WOULD
HAVE NEVER FAILED THIS TEST.

THERE IS NO EXCUSE FOR THIS, NOR AM
I TRYING TO GIVE YOU ONE.

I'VE LOOKED MYSELF IN THE FACE
AND COME TO TERMS WITH WHAT I'VE DONE.

I REALIZE WHAT I DID WAS AN INVASION
OF YOUR OWN PRIVATE SPACE.

I FELT MY WHOLE WORLD HAD ENDED
WHEN I WAS STANDING IN YOUR PLACE.

I LONG FOR YOU TO FIND A WAY
TO CARRY ON SOMEHOW.

ALTHOUGH, I KNOW IT SOUNDS SO
STRANGE I COME UP WITH THIS NOW.

SOMETIMES WE ALLOW THINGS TO
HAPPEN CAUSE WE LET SATAN RULE.

BUT BECAUSE OF THIS HERE MISHAP,
GOD PLEASE EQUIPPED ME WITH A DURABLE TOOL.

I DON'T FULLY UNDERSTAND
HOW OR WHY THIS HAD TO BE.

IT WAS A WRONG DECISION I ONCE WAS
IN BLIND BUT NOW I SEE.

I HAVE LEARNED THIS COSTLY LESSON
AND VOW NEVER TO GO BACK TO DOOM.

I JUST PRAY THAT IN YOUR HEART
FORGIVENESS YOU'LL FIND ROOM.

YOU'RE NOT ALONE

LONG BEFORE YOU EVER
THOUGHT OR KNEW
GOD SET FORTH PREPARATION FOR
THE MANY THINGS YOU MUST DO
THE PLAN AND CONSTRUCTION
FOR YOUR DESTINY WAS MADE
AND EVERY FRAGMENT OF
A DETAIL GOD PURPOSELY LAID
NOTHING IN THIS LIFE HAPPENS
BY CHANCE OR BY CHOICE
GOD SETS THE STAGE YOU
SHOULD WAIT FOR HIS VOICE
GOD WILL INSTRUCT AND
LEAD YOU DAY BY DAY
YOU JUST NEED TO LISTEN
HE WILL SHOW YOU THE WAY
DURING THIS JOURNEY AT TIMES
ON YOUR FACE YOU MAY FALL
WHEN THIS HAPPENS MAKE
GOD THE NAME YOU CALL
FOR EVERYTIME YOU NEED
HE WILL ALWAYS AVAIL
LEAN AND DEPEND ON HIM
ONLY HE NEVER FAILS
BECAUSE YOU ARE HUMAN AND
SOMETIMES HAVE DOUBT
IT IS IMPORTANT TO KNOW
A KNOWNDOWN IS NOT A KNOCKOUT

THE ALLUSION

SATAN'S COMFORTS AIN'T WORTH
LOOSING YOUR PRECIOUS SOUL OVER.

YOUR SITUATION WILL STILL BE THERE
AND YOU'LL HAVE TO FACE IT SOBER.

THAT MAN WHO'S THERE TO HOLD
AND SQUEEZE YOU ALL NIGHT LONG.

AS SOON AS DAWN CAN BREAK ON
HIS WAY HE WILL BE GONE.

LEAVING YOU IN FAR WORSE SHAPE
THAN YOU EVER WERE BEFORE.

AND BY THE TIME HE'S OUT OF SIGHT
HE'LL BE CROSSING SOMEONE ELSE'S DOOR.

WHEN YOU TAKE THAT HIT THAT FEELS
SO GOOD IT MAKES YOU WANT TO HOLLER.

JUST REMEMBER TO GET THAT FIX YOU
SOLD YOUR SOUL FOR A DOLLAR.

YOU SEE THAT GLASS, THAT PIPE,
THAT PERSON'S ARMS WILL ONLY BRING YOU DOWN.

THE ONLY THING YOU CAN COUNT ON FROM IT
IS GOD'S THRONE YOU WON'T BE AROUND.

ALL THESE SOLUTIONS ARE TEMPORARY
THE PROBLEM IS DEEPER THAN THAT.

WHEN IT'S OVER IT WILL BE WORSE
AND THAT IS A TRUE, HONEST FACT.

IF YOU ONLY WIPE THE SURFACE DEEP
INSIDE WILL ROT AND SMELL.

WHAT YOU TRIED TO CLEAN IS COVERED
BUT IF YOU SNIFF YOU CAN STILL TELL.

SATAN KNOWS YOUR WEAKNESS
AND HE USES THEM TO TEMPT.

SATAN IS A LOW DOWN DIRTY DOG, YES,
SATAN AND ALL HIS IMPS.

EVIL FORCES ARE FOR REAL AND
THEY'RE GOING TO PLAY THEIR ROLE.

THEY ARE ON ASSIGNMENT FROM THE PIT
SO GOD'S FACE YOU WON'T BEHOLD.

THEY WILL ENTICE AND SEDUCE YOU
INTO FALLING INTO SIN.

IF THEY ARE UNSUCCESSFUL THEY
WILL FIGHT YOU TO THE END.

YOU MUST KNOW THERE IS A WAR GOING ON
AND IT'S NOT A PHYSICAL FIGHT.

IT IS A SPIRITUAL WAR AND SATAN
WANTS YOUR SOUL WITH ALL HIS MIGHT.

GOD MOST CERTAINLY HAS THE UPPERHAND
SO THE ADVERSARY WILL STOOP WAY LOW.

TO CAPTURE THE VERY ESSENCE OF
YOUR SOUL AND CEASE YOUR BLESSING FLOW.

THE STRATEGIES HE USES ARE
CUNNY, PERVERSE, AND CRUEL.

YOU DON'T HAVE TO FALL PREY
TO SATAN YOU DON'T HAVE TO BE HIS FOOL.

FIGHT DEMONIC FORCES FIGHT
THEM TOOTH AND NAIL.

IF YOU DON'T THERE WILL BE A
SPECIAL PLACE FOR YOU IN HELL!

NOW WITH HIS COMFORTS THE ENEMY WILL
TEMPT YOU BUT DON'T FORGET THE PRICE YOU'LL PAY.

TURN YOUR FACE AND LOOK TO JESUS
FOR ON CALVARY HE PAID YOUR WAY.

FOR OVER THE ENEMY YOU
HAVE THE POWER TO BEAT.

TO KILL AND DESTROY SATAN'S
ARMY TO DEFEAT.

WHAT YOU SHOULD REMEMBER IS
GOD IS MIGHTER THAT HE.

HE HAS ORCHESTRATED A FOOL PROOF
PLAN TO SET THE CAPTIVES FREE.

FROM NEAR TRAGEDY TO TRIUMPH (MY TESTIMONY)

I RECALL ALONG TIME AGO, I
WAS SO VERY CLOSE TO GOD.

HE WAS THERE TO GUIDE AND COMFORT
ME JUST LIKE THE STAFF AND THE ROD.

BUT SOMETHING HAPPENED I DRIFTED OFF
AND I COULD NO LONGER HEAR.

THE VOICE THAT GUIDED ME FROM MY
BIRTH THAT I HELD IN MY HEART SO DEAR.

SIN WAS THE CULPRIT THAT LED ME
OUT OF GOD'S WILL AND INTO THE WORLD.

THE DEVIL WAS NOW THE DRIVER
AND WAS TAKING ME INTO A DOWNWARD SWIRL.

SATAN WANTED ME TO THINK THAT BECAUSE
I'D FALLEN OUT OF GOD'S OWN GRACE.

THAT I HAD LOST, TOTALLY FAILED
AND SHOULD GIVE UP ON THIS RACE.

I KNOW THAT GOD DIDN'T LEAVE ME
STANDING OUT IN THE STORM AND THE COLD.

IT WAS A TRICK OF THE ENEMY THAT
SET ME UP TO FAIL AND TO FOLD.

I WAS DECEIVED AND ENTICED BY
SATAN HIMSELF BEFORE I KNEW WHAT FELL.

THE DEVIL THOUGHT HE HAD ME
AND WAS DRAGGING ME TO HELL.

GOD SENT HIS MESSENGER TO TELL
ME I COULD REDEEM MY VERY OWN SOUL.

I COULD REPENT, LEAVE MY SINS IN
THE PAST AND END UP JUST AS PURE GOLD.

I SURRENDERED MYSELF TO CHRIST
HE WASHED ME WHITER THAN SNOW.

WITH THE BLOOD OF JESUS HE WASHED
ME JUST LIKE THE BIBLE SAYS SO.

HE MOLDED ME TRANSFORMED ME TURNED
ME INTO THE PERSON YOU SEE TODAY.

ALL WASHED UP WITH THE PAST
BEHIND NO MATTER WHAT MEN SAY.

MY HORRIED PAST
HAS BEEN ERASED.

AT LAST, I'M IN HIS WILL AND
IN MY PLACE.

MY USED TO BE HAS FORMED
THIS MINISTRY.

I WAS BROUGHT WITH
A PRICE BACK ON CALVARY.

IT'S GREAT TO BE BACK TO THE DAYS
THAT I COULD REACH OUT AND TOUCH.

MY SAVIOR, MY LORD, MY DELIVERER,
MY FRIEND AND MY CREATOR AND SUCH.

A COVENANT

WHEN IN PRAYER FOR
A SPECIFIC BLESSING
MAKE A COVENANT WITH GOD.

THIS WILL ELEVATE
ALL THE STRESSING
MAKE A COVENANT WITH GOD.

A COVENANT IS A PROMISE TO GIVE UP
SOMETHING TO GET THAT SPECIAL REQUEST.

YOU MAY HAVE TO GIVE UP ONE THING
TO GET ANOTHER THAT IS BEST.

REMEMBER IF YOU MAKE A PROMISE YOU CAN
LIVE WITH YOU WILL SURELY BE FAVORED.

YOUR FAITH WILL GROW BY LEAPS AND BOUNDS
AND WILL NEVER EVER BE WAVERED.

A COVENANT IS A PROMISE TO
EXCHANGE ONE THING FOR ANOTHER.

A COVENVANT IS MADE TO OUR SUPREME
BEING AS THERE SURELY IS NONE OTHER.

I AM LOVED

I AM LOVED BY GOD NO
MATTER WHAT OR WHEN.
UNCONDITIONAL LOVE SENT FROM
ABOVE ON HIM I CAN DEPEND.

IT MAKES NO DIFFERENCE
WHETHER I'M BAD OR GOOD.
GOD LOVES ME DEARLY EVEN
WHEN I DON'T DO AS I SHOULD.

YES, HE LOVES ME
I DON'T KNOW WHY.
BUT FOR MY SINS HE GAVE
HIS ONLY SON TO DIE.

THAT I MAY ONE DAY
WALK STREETS OF GOLD.
AND MY SAVIOR'S
FACE I SHALL BEHOLD.

GOD ALSO PROTECTS ME FROM ALL
DANGERS EVEN THE UNSEEN.
HIS EVERLASTING ARMS IS WHERE
I HAVE LEARNED TO LEAN.

THERE IS NO OTHER
GOD AS MERCIFUL AS HE.
FOREVER WILL I LOVE YOU LORD,
WITHOUT YOU WHERE WOULD I BE.

MY ONLY REQUEST

LORD DON'T LET ME STRAY FROM
THY HOLY WILL THIS IS MY ONLY REQUEST.
I WANT MY EVERY ACTION WHOLESOME
SO MY SOUL YOU WILL NOT DETEST.

I ONLY WANT TO BE HOLY
AND PLEASING IN YOUR SIGHT.
SO, I MAY HAVE YOU AROUND ME
AND BE PROTECTED BY ALL OF YOUR MIGHT.

I KNOW WITHOUT YOU DWELLING
INSIDE ME, I COULD NOT EVEN SEE.
YOUR STRENGTHS, YOUR POWER,
YOUR MAGNITUDE, NOR WOULD I EVEN BE.

MY ENTIRE EXISTENCE, ALL MY
ACCOMPLISHMENTS ARE ALL BECAUSE OF YOU.
BEFORE ME YOU HAVE WALKED MY STEPS
AND MY FAITH WILL SEE ME THROUGH.

THIS ONE REQUEST IS SO INSTRUMENTAL
AND WILL ENSURE I WON'T BE DEVOURED.
I AM MORE THAN DETERMINED TO MAKE IT
AND YOUR WILL, WILL KEEP ME EMPOWERED.

WHEN GOD CALLS . . .

QUITE OFTEN WE HEAR GOD CALLING
AND WE WONDER JUST WHAT SHOULD WE DO.
QUITE OFTEN WE HEAR GOD CALLING
AND WE ACT LIKE WE DON'T HAVE A CLUE.

FOR IF SOMEHOW IT CHANGED
AND THE ROLES WERE NOW REVERSED.
SO STRESSFUL WE WOULD SCREAM IT
WOULD TRULY SOUND REHEARSED.

PICTURE THIS A DESPARATE CHILD,
"OH GOD PLEASE HONOR MY REQUEST!"
WE WOULD EXPECT GOD TO JUMP
AND GET US THROUGH THIS TEST.

IF ONLY WHEN GOD CALLS
WE WOULD MOVE UPON DEMAND.
IF ONLY WHEN GOD CALLS
WE WOULD DO AS HE COMMANDS.

NOW WHEN WE ARE IN A SITUATION
AND NEED TO GET A PRAYER THROUGH.
REMEMBER OUR REACTION WHEN ON THE
OTHER FOOT WAS THE SHOE.

WE WOULDN'T WANT HIM TO STALL
NOR WOULD WE WANT HIM TO TARRY.
WE WOULD WANT HIM TO REACT
AND ALL OUR BURDENS FOR HIM TO CARRY.

SO NEXT TIME WHEN GOD CALLS
WE WILL DO JUST WHAT WE'RE TOLD.
SO NEXT TIME WHEN GOD CALLS
WE WILL SIT BACK AND ALLOW HIM TO MOLD.

THE POWER OF GOD

NEVER UNDER ESTIMATE THE
POWER OF GOD'S WEIGHT.

HE IS CAPABLE OF ANYTHING
AND WILL GET US TO OUR FATE.

THERE IS NOTHING HE CAN'T DO
NO MOUNTAIN HE CAN'T CLIMB.

JUST PUT YOUR TRUST IN HIM
HE'LL GET YOU THROUGH HARD TIMES.

HE IS STRONG, MIGHTY, AND HOLDS THE
WHOLE WORLD IN HIS HANDS.

HE IS JUST AS GENTLE AS HE
IS POWERFUL AND HE ALWAYS UNDERSTANDS.

NO ONE ELSE CAN MOVE ON YOUR BEHALF
THE WAY THAT MY GOD CAN.

IF YOU JUST WATCH GOD DO HIS WORK
YOU'LL SEE MIRACLES ALL OVER THIS LAND.

SO IF JESUS CAN WALK ON WATER
SURELY HE CAN GET US OUT OF OUR MESS.

SOME OF OUR DILEMMAS AND PROBLEMS
ARE LESSONS WE MUST LEARN BY A TEST.

IF GOD CAN MAKE A HIGHWAY
IN THE MIDDLE OF THE SEA.

WHY CAN'T HE STEP IN TODAY TO
DO THE SAME FOR YOU AND ME?

YOU HAVE NOT CAUSE YOU ASK NOT
SO DON'T LET THIS HAPPEN TO YOU.

ALWAYS TAKE YOUR BURDENS TO JESUS
I PROMISE HE'LL KNOW JUST WHAT TO DO.

YOU MUST BELIEVE

PRAY AND BELIEVE IN
GOD THE FATHER.

IF YOU DON'T BELIEVE
THEN DON'T EVEN BOTHER.

BELIEVING IS FAITH AND FAITH
CAN MOVE MOUNTAINS.

ABUNDANCE IS FAITH IT RAINS
ON US LIKE SPRING FOUNTAINS.

WE ARE IN CONTROL AS
TO WHETHER WE RECEIVE.

FAITH IS PLENTIFUL TO
ALL THAT DO BELIEVE.

SO NEXT TIME YOU FALL DOWN ON
YOUR KNEES TO GO IN PRAYER.

IT IS IMPERATIVE TO KNOW
THAT GOD WILL ALWAYS BE RIGHT THERE.

TRUST IN GOD ONLY

WHY WOULD I PUT MY TRUST IN
MAN WHO IS MERELY A MAN?
WHEN I HAVE A HEAVENLY FATHER
WHO IS GOD ALL BY HIMSELF.
MY POWER DOES NOT COME FROM
MAN WHO CAN'T SUPPLY HIS OWN.
MY POWER COMES FROM THE ALMIGHTY
WHOSE POWER SOURCE IS UNKNOWN.

A NEVER ENDING FLOW THAT
CARRIES US FROM BIRTH TO ETERNITY.
YES, MAN WAS CREATED IN GOD'S
OWN IMAGE BUT GOD IS AN ORIGINAL.
HE MADE US RULER OVER MANY THINGS
AND HE MADE US ABOVE ALL OTHER
LIVING CREATURES. MY HEAVENLY FATHER
IS NOT ONLY KING OF KINGS,
BUT ALSO LORD OF LORDS.

GOD CAN DO ALL THINGS LARGE
AND SMALL THERE IS NO CIRCUMSTANCE
OR SITUATION SO TOUGH THAT GOD
WOULD JUST THROWN IN THE TOWEL.
IF YOU ARE AT A CROSSROAD IN YOUR
LIFE AND YOU DON'T KNOW WHICH WAY
YOU SHOULD TO TURN. GIVE IT OVER TO GOD
ASK HIM TO LEAD YOU INTO THE PATH
OF HIS PERFECT WILL AND TRUST
THAT HE WILL DO JUST WHAT HE SAID.

GOD LOVES YOU AND HIS PERFECT WILL
IS WHERE YOU SHOULD WANT TO BE.

ALL THESE BLESSINGS

THANK YOU GOD FOR ALL THESE BLESSINGS
THAT I KNOW I DIDN'T EARN.
THANK YOU LORD FOR ALL THE BLESSINGS
AND GIFTS LIKE THE SPIRIT TO DISCERN.
THANK YOU GOD FOR ALL THESE BLESSINGS
THAT MY HEART CHERISHES SO DEARLY.
THANK YOU LORD FOR ALL THESE BLESSINGS
AND YOUR VOICE I HEAR SO CLEARLY.

FOR YOU ARE ALWAYS WITH ME
AND YOUR PRESENCE FILLS MY DAY.
I SHALL FOREVER LOVE AND EXALT
YOU IN EVERY SINGLE WAY.
THANK YOU GOD FOR ALL THESE BLESSINGS
THAT YOU SAW FIT FOR ME TO RECEIVE.
THANK YOU LORD FOR ALL THESE BLESSINGS
AND THE PROTECTION FROM ALL WHO DECEIVE.

THANK YOU GOD FOR ALL THESE BLESSINGS
AND FOR NOT LETTING MY ENEMIES SURVIVE.
THANK YOU LORD FOR ALL THESE BLESSINGS
AND FOR ALWAYS ALLOWING MY SOUL TO REVIVE.
WHENEVER I CAN'T FIND MY WAY
YOU ALWAYS INTERCEDE.
YOU ORDER MY STEPS, HOLD MY HAND,
MY PATHWAY YOU ALWAYS LEAD.

THIS IS WHY MY CONFIDENCE
BELONGS TO ONLY YOU.
BECAUSE YOU PROTECT AND GOT MY BACK
IN ALL THAT I GO THROUGH.
THERE IS NO GREATER LOVE THAN
THE ONE THAT WE BOTH SHARE.
BECAUSE YOU SHOW ME EVERYDAY THAT
YOU WILL ALWAYS BE RIGHT THERE.

WHENEVER I CLOSE MY EYES I AM
THANKFUL THAT YOU'RE NEAR.
ENFORCING YOUR HEDGE OF PROTECTION
AROUND ME SO I MAY NEVER FEAR.
ALMIGHTY AND POWERFUL IS MY GOD
WHO GAVE HIS SON'S OWN LIFE.
THAT I MIGHT HAVE SALVATION AND
NOT LIVE ETERNITY IN STRIFE.

IN LOVING MEMORY OF MY GRANDMOTHER,

ELLA MAE LONDON RICHARD PHILDELPHIA, PA
BORN IN APPALACHICOLA, FL

THE PRESENCE OF GOD

JOY IS IN THE PRESENCE OF GOD
NOT IN THE ABSENCE OF PAIN.

HE IS THE MAKER OF INDESCRIBABLE JOY
AND FOREVER HE DOES REIGN.

GLORIOUS SPLENDOR IT IS TO USHER
IN THE PRECIOUS HOLY GHOST.

HONOR IT IS TO BASK IN THE PRESENCE
OF THE BLESSED HEAVENLY HOST.

THIS IS WHERE HE LIFTS THE
VEIL OFF OUR SPIRITUAL EYES.

AND HOW WE GET STRENGTH TO ABSTAIN
WHEN OUR OWN FLESH DIES.

THERE IS ALWAYS PEACE AND HAPPINESS
IN THE CENTER OF GOD'S MIDST.

WE MUST ABSORB THIS ATMOSPHERE
SO OUR SOULS WON'T BE AT RISK.

THE MERE FRAGRANCE OF THE MASTER
WILL HEIGHTEN OUR SPIRITAL GROWTH.

THE DECLARATION OF SALVATION FROM
OUR MOUTHS WILL BOLDLY COME FORTH.

BEHOLD FOR THE GROUND WHERE YOU
STAND IS INDEED THE HOLY OF HOLY.

THE PROMISE GOD EXTENDS IS SO FIRM
YOU CAN STAND UPON IT SOLELY.

WHAT AN EXTREME MIGHTY GOD WE SERVE
WE GLORIFY HIM FOR THIS HE DESERVES.

INDULGE IN THE GREAT PLEASURE
OF HIS SANCTIFIED FORCE.

YOU MUST LET HIS POWER MANIFEST
AT ITS OWN DISTINCT COURSE.

DEDICATED TO MY AUNT

EOLA "NANNY MOORE" WINGATE MOORE

GOD'S TIMING

YOUR CONCEPTION UNLEASHED
WHAT IS DESTINED FOR YOU.
ALL YOUR TRIALS ARE PREPARATION
FOR THE THINGS YOU ARE TO PURSUE.

THE WORD TELL US WHOM GOD
CALLS HE SURELY QUALIFIES.
AND GOD IS NOT A MAN THAT
HE SHOULD TELL LIES.

ALL THINGS TO BE REVEALED
WHEN GOD SAYS THEY WILL.
SOMETIMES WE DON'T NEED TO KNOW
UNTIL GOD'S TIMING IS FULFILLED.

WAIT I SAY ON THE LORD HE
WILL RENEW YOUR STRENGTHS.
AND LET YOU KNOW EVERY DETAIL
OF YOUR DESTINY AT LENGTHS.

FINAL DESTINATION IS NOT
WHERE YOU ARE TODAY.
IT IS THE BEGINNING OF GREATNESS
IF YOU TRUST IN GOD AND OBEY.

YOUR SOUL

WE GET SO CAUGHT UP IN
OUR PHYSICAL NEEDS,
OUR SPIRITUAL WALK WITH JESUS
IS WHAT MUST TAKE THE LEAD.
NOW DON'T GET ME WRONG
OR GET MISUNDERSTOOD.
WE HAVE TO TAKE CARE OF OUR BODIES
WE REALLY KNOW WE SHOULD.
WHEN THIS LIFE IS OVER THE
PHYSICAL THINGS WILL BE LEFT BEHIND.
WHAT WE WILL TAKE WITH US
ARE THE THINGS OF A SPIRITUAL KIND.
THE ONLY THING WE HAVE LEGITIMATE
CLAIM ON IS WHAT LIES DEEP INSIDE.
SO IN ALL SITUATIONS LET YOUR
SPIRIT BE YOUR GUIDE.

YOUR SOUL DOES NOT WANT TO BE TORTURED
IN THE BURNING, SMOTHERING HEAT.
YOUR SOUL WANTS TO BE CONTENT
AND REST AT THE MASTER'S FEET.

YOUR BODY WAS MADE FOR THE WORLD
AND IT YEARNS FOR PHYSICAL PLEASURES.
WHAT'S GOOD FOR THE BODY IN THE
SPIRIT MAY TRULY BE NO TREASURE.
JUST BECAUSE IT MESMERIZES YOUR
BODY TO YOUR SOUL IT'S NOT THE SAME.
AND WHEN THE ROLL IS CALLED UP YONDER
BECAUSE OF THIS YOU WON'T FIND YOUR NAME.
TAKE CONTROL OF YOUR BODY, DON'T
LET IT CONTROL YOU IN LUST.
IN ORDER TO MAKE IT TO HEAVEN YOU MUST
BE WHOLESOME, UPRIGHT, AND JUST.

YOUR SPIRIT IS YOURS FOREVER
SO LISTEN WHEN IT SPEAKS.
IT WILL NEVER LEAD YOU WRONG CAUSE
HEAVEN'S THRONE IS WHAT IT SEEKS.

TRULY BLESSED

YOUR MERE APPEARANCE MAY NOT MAKE
OTHERS AWARE THAT YOU'RE BLESSED.
MIRACLE IT IS YOU'RE STILL BREATHING, YOU WERE
SUPPOSED TO BE WIPED OUT IN THAT LAST TEST.

SIMPLY BECAUSE GOD SAVE YOU,
YOU SHOULD HAVE A BRAND NEW ATTITUDE.
WE OWE GOD EVERYTHING AND OUR HEARTS
OVERFLOW WITH MUCH GRATITUDE.

GOD SAW FIT TO KEEP YOU AS HE IS
NOT FINISHED WITH YOU YET.
YOUR PURPOSE IS NOT QUITE FULFILLED AND YOUR
CHARACTER TRAITS ARE NOT COMPLETELY MET.

GOD WILL SHOW YOU WHAT LIES
AHEAD IN LIFE YOU'LL SEE.
IT MUST BE INSTRUMENTAL AS
THE ENEMY DOES NOT WANT IT TO BE.

JUST CONTINUE TO PRESS
AND NEVER GIVE IN.
GOD HAS YOUR BACK AND
WITH HIM YOU'LL SURELY WIN.

FREE

IN THE WIND HE WANTS
HIS ASHES TO BE BLOWN.

TO REFLECT HIS LIFE FROM
ITS MORNING TILL ITS DAWN.

ALWAYS ON THE GO TO
STOP FOR JUST A WHILE.

ALL OVER THE WORLD HE
TRAVELLED A MANY, MANY MILE.

HIGH SPIRITED AND UNTAMED DESCRIBES
MY UNCLE RO QUITE WELL.

NOTHING CAN HOLD HIM DOWN
NOT SNOW, SLEET, OR HAIL.

HIS EYES HAVE SEEN
MUCH, HIS FOOTSTEPS MANY.

HE DEARLY ENJOYS LIFE AND GOOD TIMES
HE HAS HAD PLENTY.

JUST LIKE THE WIND HE'S UNINHIBITED,
REFRESHING, AND FREE.

IF YOU HAVE OBSERVED ANY
OF HIS LIFE THEN YOU WILL SURELY SEE.

WHEN HIS TIME COMES AND YOU'RE
FULL OF GRIEF AND DOUBT.

JUST AS IN LIFE THE LONE
RANGER MUST CHECK OUT.

AFTER HE'S GONE AND
YOU FEEL THE WIND BLOW.

THERE WILL BE COMFORT IN KNOWING
MY UNCLE IS STILL ON THE GO.

DEDICATED TO MY "UNCLE RO"

ROHAVEN RICHARD, I
BALTIMORE, MD

IDOLATRY

IDOLATRY IS OF AN EARTHLY NATURE
IT STEMS FROM A PHYSICAL NEED.

SEXUAL IMMORALITY, LUST,
EVIL DESIRES, AND OF GREED.

CRUCIFY HUMAN NATURE THIS IS
PHYSICAL PASSIONS AND DESIRES.

UTILIZE THE FRUITS OF THE SPIRIT
THEY ALWAYS HELP TO INSPIRE.

THERE SHOULDN'T BE A HINT OF IDOLATRY
IN THE ONES THAT ARE TRULY SET APART.

THESE ARE THE ONES THAT ARE CHOSEN TRYING
THEIR BEST TO PLEASE GOD'S OWN HEART.

AGAINST GOD AND ONESELF IS THE
RESULT OF SEXUAL SIN.

THESE ARE THE CRIMES AGAINST ONE'S OWN FLESH
BECAUSE THEY ARE DONE WITHIN.

DRUG ABUSE IS ANOTHER SIN THAT IS
DONE UNTO YOUR OWN TEMPLE.

TO ELEVATE THESE SINS YOU SHOULD JUST ABSTAIN
ALTHOUGH SOMETIMES IT'S NOT QUITE THAT SIMPLE.

PUT YOUR HUMAN NATURE UNDER SUBJECTION
THIS HAS TO BE DONE EVERYDAY.

TAKE ALL OF YOUR BURDENS TO JESUS AND LEAVE
THEM AS THIS IS WHERE THEY SHOULD LAY.

HELP

I HAVE JUMPED IN FRONT OF GOD TRYING
TO HANDLE THINGS ON MY OWN ACCORD

I HAVE STEPPED RIGHT OUT THERE
WITHOUT HIS CONSENT
NOW I CAN'T GET MY REWARDS.

LORD, LOOK AT THE MESS I'VE
MADE THAT ONLY YOU CAN FIX.

NOW I NEED ASSISTANCE WHEN I
SHOULD HAVE WAITED FOR YOU INSTEAD.

YOU KNOW I KNOW BETTER THAN THIS
I GUESS I'M MAKING MYSELF A HARD BED.

LORD, LOOK AT THE MESS
I'VE MADE THAT ONLY YOU CAN FIX.

ON THIS JOURNEY IN LIFE SOMETIMES
WE FIND OURSELVES JUMPING OUT AHEAD.

REMEMBER, GOD IS QUITE CAPABLE OF
LEADING, JUST LIKE WE KNOW HE SAID.

LORD, LOOK AT THE MESS I'VE
MADE THAT ONLY YOU CAN FIX.

NOW I REALIZE TO MAKE IT
I MUST NOT GET IN GOD'S WAY.

I KNOW I CAN'T GET IMPATIENT
I MUST BE REAL STILL AND STAY.

THANK YOU LORD FOR THE MESS I'VE MADE
THAT ONLY YOU CAN FIX.

THANK YOU GOD FOR THIS LESSON I
LEARNED THAT YOU HAD ALREADY HAD IN THE MIX.

SALVATION

THIS MAY BE THE ONLY BIBLE YOU READ SO
I'VE GOT TO GET THIS MESSAGE THROUGH
GOD SENT HIS ONLY SON JESUS TO PAY THE
PRICE FOR ME AND YOU

GOD KNEW WE WOULD BE TEMPTED
AND FALL SHORT OF THE GLORY I'M TOLD
SO HE MAPPED OUT A PLAN FOR SALVATION
SO WE COULD HAVE ANOTHER CHANCE TO BEHOLD

IF YOU CONFESS WITH YOUR MOUTH AND
BELIEVE THAT JESUS PAID YOUR COST
THIS IS THE SOLUTION GOD CAME UP WITH
TO MAKE CERTAIN YOUR SOUL WON'T BE LOST

SEEK YE FIRST THE KINGDOM OF GOD
AND ALL ELSE SHALL COME TO YOU
PUT GOD FIRST IN EVERYTHING AND ASK
HIS ASSISTANCE IN ALL YOUR PURSUE

WHEN THIS PART IS COMPLETE
AND THIS PART IS DONE
DELIVERANCE IS THE NEXT
THING WE'LL ASK OF THE SON

MY ASSIGNMENT

THERE IS A TASK THAT
LIES AHEAD THAT ONLY I CAN DO.
I PLAY A ROLE WITHOUT A MASK
FOR MY IDENTITY MUST BE TRUE.

GOD EQUIPS ME WITH HIS GREAT POWER
AND THE STRENGTH TO MAKE IT BACK.
MY CONFIDENCE IS QUITE STRONG SO
SATAN CAN'T TAKE ME IN A SUDDEN ATTACK.

THERE ARE TRULY SOME SOULS WAITING
FOR GOD'S WORD TO COME THROUGH ME.
TO STAND STILL WOULD HOLD UP PROGRESS
OR WHAT HAS BEEN ORDAINED BY THEE.

THEIR BLOOD WILL BE ON MY HANDS
IF I NEVER BECOME WHAT GOD CALLED.
I REALLY KNOW I HAVE TO DO THIS
OR MY SIBLINGS MAY TAKE THE FALL.

HOW SMALL SHALL THE THINGS BE
THAT WERE STANDING IN MY WAY.
WHEN I BOW BEFORE THE LORD ON
THAT LAST AND FINAL DAY.

TO BE PLEASING IN YOUR SIGHT
IS ALL I WANT TO DO.
SO THAT MY ENTIRE LIFE WILL
ONLY COUNT FOR YOU.

I WILL HOLD UP MY LIGHT AND
NOT LET SATAN STEAL YOUR GLORY!
I WILL COMPLETE MY ASSIGNMENT
THERE IS NO NEED TO WORRY.

AS LONG AS GOD IS FOR ME
I SHALL MAKE IT TO THE END.
I WANT TO BE USED TO UPLIFT THEE
AND THE WAR AGAINST THE ENEMY TO WIN!

DEDICATED TO ALL READERS OF THIS BOOK.

JOYCE RICHARD MONTGOMERY,
MINISTER, POET AND AUTHOR

HOMELESS

IF I WERE HOMELESS WOULD
YOU STOP AND LEND A HAND.
OR WOULD YOU GIVE ME THAT LOOK
TO MAKE ME HIDE MY FACE IN THE SAND.

IF I WERE HOMELESS DON'T EVEN
THINK I PLANNED ON THIS.
I DON'T THINK ANYONE WOULD
DREAM OF BEING ON THE HOMELESS LIST.

HOMELESS IS A SITUATION THAT MANY
ARE JUST A PAYCHECK FROM.
SO DON'T THINK I AM TRIFLING
OR THINK I'M JUST A BUM.

I AM A HUMAN BEING WITH
NEEDS AND FEELINGS, TOO.
I'M JUST IN BETWEEN BLESSINGS BUT
IF I COULD I WOULD BLESS YOU.

IMAGINE IF YOU WERE ME
AND HAD NO HOME AT ALL.
NOR HAD NO FRIENDS OR FAMILY
THAT YOU COULD GIVE A CALL.

I WONDER IF YOU SAW ME
RESTING ON A PARK BENCH.
WOULD YOU ACT LIKE I WAS INVISIBLE
WITHOUT THE LEST LITTLE FINCH.

I AM A REGULAR PERSON A "HELLO"
OR A SMILE WOULD BE NICE.
THAT SHOULD COME SO NATURAL YOU
SHOULDN'T HAVE TO EVEN THINK TWICE.

SO WHEN YOU SEE SOMEONE HOMELESS
REMEMBER THAT COULD HAVE BEEN YOU.
EXTEND YOUR HAND IN ASSISTANCE YOU'LL
BE BLESSED INDEED IF YOU DO.

GOD'S CREATION

I AM WHO I AM BECAUSE
GOD MADE ME THIS WAY.
SHAPED AND MOLDED BY
THE POTTER AS I AM THE CLAY.

JUST BECAUSE YOU
DON'T UNDERSTAND ME.
I AM WHO I AM BECAUSE
HE WANTED THIS TO BE.

WE ARE DIFFERENT BECAUSE
OUR CALLING ARE UNIQUE.
YOUR CALLING REQUIRES BOLDNESS
AND MINES REQUIRES MEEK.

ALL THINGS WERE CREATED
FOR AND BY ONLY HIM.
TO ENSURE HIS DIVINE VICTORY
THIS IS NOT A WHIM.

LOVE ME FOR WHO I AM
FOR YOU I'LL DO THE SAME.
THEN WE WILL WORK TOGETHER
TO GLORIFY HIS NAME.

WHAT'S YOUR CHOICE?

THE WORLD WILL MAKE YOU FEEL . . .
DISGUSTING, FLITHY, NASTY, CONDEMNED, UNWORTHLY,
USELESS, USED, UNHOLY, UNSAVED,
STUPID, UNREACHABLE,
AND UNFORGIVABLE JUST TO NAME A FEW.

GOD WILL MAKE YOU FEEL . . .
PURE, CLEANSED, WHOLESOME, SAINTLY, A VESSEL,
INSTRUMENTAL, HOLY, SAVED, AN AUTHORITY, UPLIFTED,
AND SAINTIFIED JUST TO SAY THE LEAST

NOW SINCE WE ALL KNOW GOD IS
A JEALOUS GOD AND YOU
CAN'T SERVE TWO MASTERS, YOUR ETERNITY WILL BE
DETERMINED BY THE CHOICES MADE IN THIS LIFE. MAKE
CERTAIN YOUR CHOICE IS CLEARLY GOD!!!

MY ESCAPE

MOST GRACIOUS PRAISES TO
THE LOVER OF MY SOUL,
I FEEL YOUR LOVE SO CLEARLY.
I CRY OUT TO YOU IN
A LOUD SOUND,
I HEAR YOUR
VOICE SO VIVIDLY.
IN THEE I DO
PUT ALL MY TRUST.
HOW I NEED YOUR
PRESENCE SO ANXIOUSLY,
ONLY YOU CAN PROVIDE
A WAY OF ESCAPE,
I FEEL YOUR TOUCH
SO WARMLY,
SO I WAIT WITHOUT A
SOUND FOR YOU TO MOVE.
I FEEL YOUR
PROTECTION SO STRONGLY.
FOR IN THEE I DO PUT ALL MY TRUST.

ADDICTION

WHATEVER YOUR ADDICTION IS YOU
MUST REALIZE IT IS SATANICALLY ASSIGNED.

TO CRIPPLE YOU, TO CONFUSE YOU,
AND YOUR SPIRITUAL FOCUS IT WANTS TO BIND.

AN ADDICTION IS A HINDRANCE
THAT CHOKES YOUR EVERY DREAM.

IT TAKES ON A FORM OF ITS OWN IT
CONSUMES YOUR WHOLE LIFE IT SEEMS.

IT'S ALL A BIG ALLUSION TO TAKE YOU
OFF THE ROAD YOU SHOULD TRAVEL.

IT'S SET UP TO DESTROY YOU AND
YOUR LIFE IT WANTS TO UNRAVEL.

ADDICTIONS ARE SET UPS FROM THE PIT
TO KEEP YOU FROM DOING WHAT'S RIGHT.

IT IS A TACTIC OF THE SPIRITUAL REALM
WAR AGAINST THE DARKNESS AND LIGHT.

DESPERATELY SEEK GOD TO
INTERCEDE ON YOUR BEHALF.

TO BE CERTAIN THE ADVERSARY WILL
NOT GET THE LAST LAUGH.

SOMEWHERE IN TIME

THERE IS AN ANTICIPATION OF
THE BIRTH OF YOUR CHILD.
TO FINALLY BEHOLD ITS FACE
AND SEE ITS PRECIOUS SMILE.
LONGING TO SEE WHAT LOVE HAS
MADE AND FORMED INSIDE OF YOU.
A LIFE, A GIFT BROUGHT TO THIS
WORLD JUST TO NAME A FEW.
YOU WILL NOT KNOW AGAPE LOVE
UNTIL THIS CHILD COMES TO BE.
IT'S HARD TO BELIEVE SOMEWHERE IN
TIME SOMEONE FELT THIS WAY ABOUT ME.

KNOWING YOUR NEEDS WILL BE CARED
FOR EVERY TIME YOU CRY.
FEELING SOMEONE LOVES YOU BECAUSE
YOU'RE THEIR BABY, THAT'S WHY.
LOVING SOMEONE ALREADY OF
WHOM YOU HAVE NEVER MET.
KNOWING THAT AS LONG AS THEY'RE
ALIVE YOU WILL NEVER HAVE TO FRET.
THIS CHILD WILL TEACH YOU MORE
THAN YOUR EYES WILL EVER SEE.
IT'S HARD TO BELIEVE SOMEWHERE IN
TIME SOMEONE FELT THIS WAY ABOUT ME.

HOLDING ON TO EACH MOMENT
AS IF IT WERE YOUR LAST.
WONDERING WHETHER TO GO ON TO
THE FUTURE OR TO REMAIN THERE IN THE PAST.
WANTING THE BEST FOR THIS PERSON AND
NOT EVER WANTING TO LET GO.
BUT KNOWING DEEP DOWN IN YOUR

HEART YOU REALLY MUST DO SO.
YOUR LOVE WILL TRULY TEACH THIS
CHILD FAR MORE THAN HIS EYES CAN SEE.
THIS MAKES ME KNOW SOMEWHERE IN TIME
SOMEONE FELT THIS WAY ABOUT ME.

IT COULD HAVE BEEN ME

WHEN I HEAR OF CHILDREN BEING
MOLESTED BY SOMEONE THE FAMILY KNOWS,
VIOLATING A CHILD IS WRONG NO
MATTER WHICH WAY IT GOES.
TO HURT A CHILD IN ANYWAY,
YOUR MIND HAS TO BE TWISTED.
WE MUST PROTECT ALL CHILDREN, IN
FACT THIS HAS TO BE INSISTED.

A CHILD'S MIND IS A PRECIOUS THING THAT
SHOULD BE LOVED AND NURTURED.
NOT USED IN A PREVERTED WAY THAT
WILL ALLOW THEIR MINDS TO BE MURDERED.
GOD BLESS THE CHILD WHO LANDS
SOMEHOW INSIDE OF DANGEROUS ARMS.
GOD PUT YOUR PROTECTION OVER
THEM AND SHIELD THEM FROM ALL HARM.

BECAUSE MISTREATED CHILDREN
ADULTS THEY'LL ONE DAY BE.
THEY ARE ALWAYS IN MY PRAYERS
BECAUSE THEY COULD HAVE BEEN ME.

A MEANINGLESS EVENT TO YOU COULD
DAMAGE THE MIND OF A CHILD.
THIS COULD EFFECT THE REST OF THEIR LIFE
TO THE POINT IT COULD MARK THEIR STYLE.
JUST ONE BAD INCIDENT COULD RUIN
THEIR WHOLE POTENTIAL.
WE MUST LOOK OUT FOR ALL CHILDREN
AND THE EXISTENCE OF THEIR CREDENTIALS.

FROM DANGERS SEEN AND UNSEEN,
FROM SEA TO SHINING SEA.
WE MUST PROTECT OUR CHILDREN
SO THAT ONE DAY THEY WILL BE

THE NEXT GENERATION TO DO THEIR
PART FOR WHATEVER IT IS WORTH.
THAT THEY CAN MAKE A DIFFERENCE
TO ALL THAT'S ON THIS EARTH.

BECAUSE MISTREATED CHILDREN
ADULTS THEY'LL ONE DAY BE.
THEY ARE ALWAYS IN MY PRAYERS
BECAUSE THEY COULD HAVE BEEN ME.

NO COINCIDENCE

THERE ARE NO COINCIDENCES AND
NOTHING IS JUST BECAUSE.
ALL THINGS HAVE A PURPOSE
I KNOW IT REALLY DOES.
THE REASON FOR ALL SITUATIONS
LIE FAR BEYOND A CHANCE.
TO TEACH, TO SHOW, AND TO ENLIGHT
OUR LIVES WILL BE ENHANCED.
THERE IS A GREATER PICTURE
THAT WE MORTAL JUST CAN'T SEE.
ALTHOUGH WE HAVE SOME UNDERSTANDING
TO A CERTAIN MINUTE DEGREE.
IT'S FAR BEYOND OUR MIND SET AND
WAY BEYOND OUR REACHES.
BUT THE LESSONS SERVE THEIR
PURPOSE AND CHARACTER IT TEACHES.
WHY DO YOU THINK YOUR TRUCK
STOPPED WHILE IT WAS STILL IN GEAR.
WHY WEREN'T YOU INSTANTLY KILLED WHEN
THAT CAR HIT YOU FROM THE REAR.
YOUR BRAINS SHOULD HAVE BEEN SCATTERED
ALL OVER THE FRONT WINDSHIELD.
BUT GOD SAW FIT TO KEEP YOU AND
NONE OF YOUR BLOOD WAS SPILLED.
GIVE THANKS TO GOD ALMIGHTY
WITH NO SUCH LUCK OF THE DRAW.
FOR WHAT HE DID FOR YOU THAT DAY,
ONLY YOU KNOW WHAT YOU SAW.

PEACE BE THINE

WHEN SOMEONE DIES THEY HAD TO GO,
THEY SIMPLY NEEDED PEACE.
WE LOVE THEM SO BUT THEY NEEDED REST
THEREFORE WE SHOULD RELEASE.
YES, THIS MAY BE THE HARDEST
THING YOU' LL EVER HAVE TO DO.
TO SET FREE SOMEONE WHO'S HOLDING
ON JUST BECAUSE OF YOU.
TO STAY FOR THEM JUST ONE MORE DAY
WILL CAUSE MORE HURT THAN GOOD.
TO MAKE IT EASIER FOR THEM JUST LET
GO WE KNOW WE REALLY SHOULD.
STAYING HERE WILL CAUSE MORE PAIN THAN
THEY WOULD EVER HAVE TO FEEL.
TO US THEY'RE PASSING ON SOMEHOW
SEEMS AN UNFAIR DEAL.
BECAUSE WE ARE LOOKING FROM
ONLY OUR OWN STAND POINT OF VIEW.
IF THE ROLES HAD BEEN REVERSED
WHAT WOULD WE REALLY DO?
WE MUST REALIZE IN THIS LIFE WHEN
THE TIME COMES WE HAVE TO LEAVE.
BECAUSE OUR DAYS ARE NUMBERED
THIS IS WHAT I DO BELIEVE.
WHEN NEAR THE END OF THE BATTLE
GOD SAYS PEACE BE THINE.
THERE IS COMFORT IN KNOWING
PEACE IS WHAT YOU'LL FIND.

TO MOMMA

THERE IS NO WAY I COULD BE THE WOMAN I AM
TODAY IF I WERE NEVER YOUR BABY GIRL.
YOU EQUIP ME WITH THE STRENGTH TO MAKE IT
IN THIS CRUEL, WICKED WORLD.
YOU INTRODUCED ME TO JESUS
AND HIS EVERLASTING ARMS.
TO PROTECT ME, WATCH OVER ME,
AND KEEP ME FROM ALL HARM.
NOT ONLY DID YOU TELL ME BUT YOU
ASSURED ME GOD WILL ANSWER WHEN I CALL.
THAT I COULD CLIMB ALL MOUNTAINS
NO MATTER HOW WIDE OR TALL.

EVEN WHEN THE ODDS WHERE AGAINST ME,
YOU ASSURED ME I COULD GO ON.
YOUR FAVORITE QUOTE TO TELL ME IS
"IT'S ALWAYS DARKEST BEFORE DAWN.
EVEN WHEN I WAS UNCERTAIN MYSELF,
YOU WOULDN'T LET ME QUIT.
YOU ALWAYS MADE ME FEEL SPECIAL
EVEN WHEN I DIDN'T SEEM TO FIT.
WHEN MY CLOUDS HUNG LOW AND
MY SKIES HAD TURNED SO GRAY.
YOU TOLD ME TO HOLD ON,
I WOULD SEE A BRIGHTER DAY.

AND WHEN I DIDN'T KNOW WHETHER
I LOVED MYSELF AT ALL.
I KNEW I LOVED YOU, BECAUSE YOU
WERE THERE WHENEVER I DID FALL.
IF ONLY MY CHILDREN WOULD LOVE
ME JUST AS HALF AS I DO YOU.
I WOULD FEEL SO SATISFIED,
MY SOUL WOULD BE BRAND NEW.
TO IMPACT SOMEONE'S LIFE SO
MUCH IS SURELY HEAVEN SENT.

JOYCE IS EVELYN'S ONLY DAUGHTER
AND I KNOW THAT THIS WAS MEANT.

YOU ARE MY QUEEN FOREVER
AND WIND BENEATH MY WING.
IF YOU HAD NOT BEEN BY MOTHER,
I WOULDN'T HAVE DONE A THING.

DEDICATED TO MY LOVING MOTHER

EVELYN WINGATE RICHARD
PENSACOLA, FL

MEMORIES OF DADDY

I REMEMBER THE TIME WE SPENT
SWINGING,
PLAYING, TALKING, LAUGHING, AND
SINGING.

WE LOVED EACH OTHER SO
STRONGLY
THAT WILL NEVER STOP.
AND YES I'M STILL YOUR
YOUR SWEET CHOCOLATE DROP.

IT'S BEEN 26 YEARS AND THE PAIN STILL
HURTS JUST LIKE IT DID WAY BACK WHEN.
WHY DID YOU GO? WHY DID YOU LEAVE?
I'VE ASKED MYSELF THIS OVER AGAIN.

I HAD PLANS FOR US, DADDY, BIG PLANS
FOR US DADDY THIS JUST CAN'T BE REAL.
WAKE UP DADDY PLEASE THIS IS TOO
MUCH FOR A CHILD MY AGE TO FEEL.

THE PAIN IS TRULY INDESCRIBABLE
I'VE GOT TO FIND A WAY TO ESCAPE.
GOD PLEASE LET ME BE DREAMING
AND SOMEONE MAKE ME AWAKE.

BUT EVERY TIME I WAS AWAKEN THIS
NIGHTMARE CONTINUED TO BE.
HOW CAN I FINISH GROWING WITHOUT
YOU?
THIS IS JUST TOO MUCH FOR ME!

I THOUGHT YOU WOULD BE HERE
FOR A MUCH LONGER TIME.
I THOUGHT YOU WOULD TEACH
MY CHILDREN OUR FAVORITE NURSERY RHYME.

DADDY, GOOD NIGHT
DADDY, SLEEP TIGHT
DADDY, I STILL LOVE YOU
WITH ALL OF MY MIGHT!

YOU SAW ALL MY BROTHERS
GROW UP AND BE TOUGH.
I DIDN'T HAVE YOU BUT ALMOST
12 YEARS WHEN GOD SAID ENOUGH.

I KNOW YOU WERE SICK
AND TIRED OF THE PAIN.
YOU CRIED OUT FOR HELP AND
GOD CALLED YOUR NAME.

IN LOVING MEMORY OF MY DEAREST DADDY

REV. DAVID RICHARD, SR
PENSACOLA, FL
OCTOBER 13,1928-JANUARY 5, 1977

YOUR WAY HOME

AT TIMES WE FIND OURSELVES
BACKED INTO A TIGHT JAM.

WHEN GOD COMES TO THE RESCUE
LIKE THE SHEPARD AND THE LOST LAMB.

THE LORD IS EVER SO BRILLIANT,
MIGHTY AND RULER OF US ALL.

AT LEAST WHEN THIS THING HAPPENS
WE KNOW JUST WHO TO CALL.

IF FOR SOME REASON AWAY
FROM SAFETY YOU ROAM.

WHAT'S IMPORTANT IS YOU
FIND YOUR WAY HOME!

SOME TIMES THE GRASS LOOKS GREENER
ON THE OTHER SIDE OF THE ROAD.

IT SEEMS THAT IT IS EASIER CAUSE SOMEONE
ELSE IS CARRYING THE LOAD.

IF YOU STEP OUT ON YOUR OWN WITHOUT
GETTING GOD'S APPROVAL.

GO TO HIM WHEN YOU NEED AWAY
BACK,
HE WILL RELEASE YOUR REMOVAL.

SO IF FOR SOME REASON AWAY
FROM SAFETY YOU ROAM.

WHAT'S IMPORTANT IS YOU ALWAYS
FIND YOUR WAY HOME!

YOUR FATE

WHAT IF THIS WERE THE HOUR HE
CAME BACK LIKE A THIEF IN THE NIGHT?

IN HIS MAJESTY, HIS SPLENDOR,
AND GLORY SHINING, OH SO BRIGHT!

ARE YOU READY OR WOULD YOU
RUN TO TRY TO REPENT REAL QUICK?

THIS WON'T WORK CAUSE IN YOUR LIFE
YOU SHOWED JUST WHO YOU PICKED?

NOAH DID NOT WAIT TILL IT WAS RAINING
FOR HIM TO BUILD THE ARK.

NEITHER SHOULD YOU WAIT TO PUT
YOUR SINFUL NATURE IN HARK.

GOD SAYS MAN WILL NOT KNOW THE
DAY NOR THE HOUR HE SHALL APPEAR.

SO YOU BETTER MAKE YOUR RESERVATION
WITH GOD SO YOU WILL HAVE NO FEAR.

FEAR IS NOT OF GOD ANYWAY IF ITS
THERE THEN YOU'RE NOT SURE.

IT WILL NOT BOTHER YOU AT ALL IF
YOU KNOW NOW THAT YOU'RE PURE.

THE PREPARATION TIME IS NOW SO
TAKE A STAND BEFORE IT TO LATE.

CAUSE IF YOU DRAG YOUR FEET TOO
LONG IT WILL ONLY MARK YOUR FATE.

BLESSINGS

BLESSINGS ARE ASSIGNED TO PLACES BE IN
THE RIGHT PLACE AT THE RIGHT TIME.
THERE ARE BLESSINGS DESIGNED FOR YOU
SO BE IN ORDER AND YOU WILL FIND.

GOD WILL DIRECT YOU TO GO RIGHT
WHERE HE LEFT YOUR SURPRISE.
BUT IF YOU MOVE TO FAST OR SLOW
THAT WHEN PROBLEMS MAY ARISE.

JUST LIKE THE LADY AT THE WELL
WAS SENT THERE TO MEET THE KING.
AND JESUS CAME TO THIS EARTH
FOR US SALVATION BRING.

WHEN GOD TOLD ELIJAH TO GO
WHERE THE RAVENS WOULD PROVIDE.
ELIJAH RECEIVED HIS BLESSING
AS GOD WAS HIS ONLY GUIDE.

GOD KNOW THE FINAL OUTCOME
BEFORE THE BEGINNING STARTS
THEN HE REVEALS IT TO US BUT
HE DOES THIS ALL IN PARTS.

THE LADY WHO DECIDED TO
PREPARE A MEAL, EAT, THEN DIE.
WAS SENT BY GOD TO GATHER STICKS
AND FIND HER ENDLESS SUPPLY.

AFTER SHE FEED THE ONE GOD SENT
THERE TO MEET HER THAT DAY,
HER CUPBOARDS WERE NEVER BARE
AGAIN IS WHAT THE BIBLE SAYS.

IF SHE HAD NOT FOLLOWED INSTRUCTIONS
SHE WOULD HAVE MET HER DEMISE.
CAUSE SHE WOULD NOT HAVE BEEN IN
PLACE TO RECEIVE HER GREAT SURPRISE.

BLESSINGS ARE ASSIGNED TO PLACES MAKE
SURE YOU'RE WHERE YOU SHOULD.
CAUSE IF YOU ARE LINE UP WITH GOD
IT WILL ONLY BE FOR YOUR GOOD.

RIGHT/WRONG

HAVE YOU EVER BEEN ON A DATE
AND EXPECTED A FAVOR IN RETURN.
IF YOU JUST PAY CLOSE ATTENTION A
VALUABLE LESSON YOU WILL LEARN.

IF YOU HAVE DATED SOMEONE
ONLY TO GET A BILL PAID.
OR YOU HAVE DONE A FAVOR TO
COVER A DEBT YOU HAD MADE.

I'M HERE TO TELL YOU THIS IS WRONG
AND THIS YOU SHOULD NOT REPEAT.
CAUSE THE OLD SAYING JUST AIN'T TRUE,
"ALL PROSTITUTES DON'T WALK THE STREETS."

IF YOUR BABY NEEDS A PAIR OF SHOES
OR SOME DIAPERS TO COVER HIS BUTT,
TO SPEND SOMETIME WITH THAT MAN
WON'T GET YOU OUT OF THIS RUT.

YOU WOULDN'T PUT A BANDAGE
ON A CUT THAT REQUIRES STITCHES.
NOR WOULD YOU POUR HOT GREASE
ON A RASH THAT REALLY ITCHES.

I'M HERE TO TELL YOU THIS IS WRONG
AND THIS YOU SHOULD NOT REPEAT.
CAUSE THE OLD SAYING JUST AIN'T TRUE,
"ALL PROSTITUTES DON'T WALK THE STREETS."

JUST BECAUSE EVERYONE'S DOING IT,
IT DOESN'T MAKE WRONG RIGHT
JUST BECAUSE EVERYONE'S DOING IT,
DON'T COMPLETELY LOSE YOUR SIGHT

IF YOU DIDN'T KNOW BEFORE
I'M SURE YOU'VE GOT THE HINT.
YOUR BODY IS A TEMPLE NOW
GO TO GOD AND REPENT.

HE IS WILLING TO FORGIVE
A MULTITUDE OF SIN.
AND IT DOESN'T MATTER WHAT
OR WHERE YOU'VE BEEN.

GOD WILL SUPPLY ALL YOUR
NEEDS JUST GO TO HIM AND ASK.
HE WILL COVER ALL OUR SINS
THEN HE'LL REMOVE OUR MASK.

BY NOW YOU KNOW THAT THIS IS
WRONG AND YOU WILL NEVER REPEAT.
CAUSE YOU KNOW FIRST HAND "ALL
PROSTITUTES DON'T WALK THE STREET."

BE GRATEFUL

BE GRATEFUL FOR DIRTY CLOTHES BECAUSE
ATLEAST YOU HAVE SOMETHING TO WEAR.
BE GRATEFUL FOR YOUR SPOUSE BECAUSE
YOU HAVE SOMEONE FOR THIS LIFE TO SHARE.

BE GRATEFUL FOR YOUR OLD MODEL CAR
BECAUSE ATLEAST YOU DON'T HAVE TO WALK.
BE GRATEFUL FOR YOUR HUSKY VOICE
BECAUSE ATLEAST YOU ARE ABLE TO TALK.

BE GRATEFUL FOR A SINK FULL OF DISHES
BECAUSE THAT'S PROOF YOUR FAMILY'S FED.
BE GRATEFUL FOR THAT LUMPY OLD MATTRESS
BECAUSE ATLEAST YOU HAVE A BED.

BE GRATEFUL FOR THE RAIN
BECAUSE AGAIN THE SUN WILL SHINE.
BE GRATEFUL FOR YOUR HEALTH,
STRENGTH, AND FOR HAVING A SOUND MIND.

BE GRATEFUL FOR THAT LEAKY ROOF
FOR ATLEAST YOU HAVE A HOME.
AS IT COULD HAVE BEEN YOU OUT
THERE IN THE STREETS TO LIVE AND ROAM.

INSTEAD OF ALWAYS COMPLAINING BE THANKFUL
THAT THINGS ARE AS BEST AS THEY ARE.
FOR COMPLAINING WON'T GET YOU ANYWHERE
AND WILL KEEP YOUR SUCCESS AT A FAR.

WHEN...

WHEN A WOMAN'S HUSBAND DIES THEN SHE'S A WIDOW
WHEN A MAN'S WIFE DIES IT MAKES HIM A WIDOWER
WHEN A CHILD'S PARENTS DIE THAT
MAKES HIM AN ORPHAN
BUT WHAT IN THE WORLD IS A MOM OR A
DAD WHEN THEIR CHILD DIES?
THERE IS NO LABEL FOR THIS BECAUSE IT SEEMS
UNNATURAL & IT IS JUST TO AWFUL
FOR PRIOR THOUGHT.

STAND FIRM

WHEN ARE WE GOING TO STOP ACCOMMODATING
THE NON-BELIEVERS IN THIS WORLD?

WHERE IS ALL THIS GOING? WHY CAN'T THEY SEE?
THIS IS GOING IN A DOWNWARD SWIRL!

SOMEONE TOOK PRAYER OUT OF THE SCHOOLS,
NOW THEY WANT GOD OUT OF THE PLEDGE.

THIS IS SATAN STRATEGY TO RULE AND IS
JUST THE BEGINNING OF THE WEDGE.

TO GOD GIVE GLORY ALWAYS
AND ALL HIS PRAISES SING.

SATAN'S TRYING TO SEPARATE US
FROM THE ONE AND ONLY KING.

YOU HOLD THE POWER, YES,
YOU HOLD THE KEY.

AT THE MENTION OF HIS NAME
THE DEMONS HAVE TO FLEE.

I DON'T KNOW HOW THEY THINK THEY
GOT HERE OR DO THEY THINK AT ALL.

BUT I KNOW MY GOD ANSWERS
EVERY SINGLE TIME I CALL.

WHAT WILL THEY WANT NEXT TO CLOSE
THE CHURCH OR JESUS NAME TO BAND.

WHATEVER IT IS, IT'S FROM THE PIT
IS WHERE THEY GOT THEIR PLAN.

WE ARE ONE NATION UNDER GOD AND
ONE NATION ON THIS EARTH.

GOD IS THE AUTHOR OF OUR FATE AND
FORMED US PRIOR TO OUR BIRTH.

SO DON'T TAKE THIS BATTLE SITTING DOWN
STAND FIRM ON THE BATTLEFIELD.

THE REWARD IS WELL WORTH YOUR WHILE
FOR ON YOU GOD'S PLACED HIS SEAL.

DADDY-DAUGHTER BOND

WHEN A DADDY TREATS HIS DAUGHTER LIKE
A PRINCESS, A QUEEN SHE'LL ONE DAY BE.

HERSELF WORTH WILL BE WHERE IT SUPPOSED TO
BECAUSE HE HAS GIVEN HER THE KEY.

TELL HER SHE IS MOST SPECIAL AND
PRECIOUS IN EVERY WAY.

TELL HER SHE IS A PERFECT GIFT NO
MATTER WHAT ANYONE SAYS.

SOME WOMEN FEEL LIKE THEY'RE NOTHING
BECAUSE NO ONE EVER TOLD THEM THEY WERE.

MAKE CERTAIN SHE KNOW HOW MUCH YOU
LOVE HER SO TO HER THIS WILL NEVER OCCUR.

DADDIES TREAT YOUR DARLING DAUGHTER
JUST AS A LADY SHOULD.

IF YOU DON'T SHE MAY ACCEPT SOMETHING
THAT MAY NOT BE FOR HER GOOD.

IF DADDIES TREAT DAUGHTERS LIKE
THE PRECIOUS JEWELS THEY ARE.

THEY WILL STRIVE EVEN HARDER AND
EXCEED THEIR EXPECTATIONS BY FAR.

DADDIES MAKE SURE YOUR DAUGHTERS
KNOW THEY DON'T HAVE TO TAKE NO MESS

AND LET HER KNOW FOR CERTAIN
SHE DESERVES THE VERY BEST.

TELL HER SHE IS ONE OF A KIND
LIKE A PRECIOUS PEARL

THEN SHE'LL KNOW WITHOUT A DOUBT
SHE'S DADDY'S BABY GIRL.

A DADDY-DAUGHTER SPECIAL BOND GIVE THE
DAUGHTER THE FOUNDATION SHE NEEDS.

SO WHEN OPPORTUNITY COMES A KNOCKING
SHE'LL BE ABLE TO SORT OUT THE WEEDS.

THORN IN MY FLESH

THIS THORN IN MY FLESH THAT
DOESN'T MIND DOING WRONG.
EVERYTIME IT DOES I END UP
SINGING THE SAME SAD SONG.

LORD, I HAVE TRIED EVERYTHING
TO MAKE IT DISAPPEAR.
I DON'T EVEN WANT IT TO EXIST
IN THIS SAME ATMOSPHERE.

IT REALLY DOES DIGUST ME I HAVE
TO REBUKE MY VERY OWN FLESH!
WITH MY DESTINY IN FRONT OF ME,
HOW HARD IT MAKES MY QUEST.

I DEVELOPED THIS OVER THE YEARS,
THIS TASTE IS TRULY ACQUIRED.
BELIEVE ME, YES, I AM QUITE ILL
OF BEING SICK AND TIRED.

IT IS SOMEWHAT PROVOCATIVE,
YET, IT KEEPS ME VERY HUMBLE.
ONLY FOR THIS FACT, LORD, PLEASE
FORGIVE ME WHEN I GRUMBLE.

THIS MESSENGER FROM SATAN
WANTS TO GIVE ME NO RELIEF.
NO MATTER WHAT HE DOES
HE DEFINITELY WON'T SWAY MY BELIEFS.

JUST LIKE PAUL IT TORMENTS ME
SOMETIMES BOTH DAY AND NIGHT.
THIS WEAKNESS IS TRULY DISTRACTING
AND AT TIMES AFFECTS MY SIGHT.

THIS THORN IN MY FLESH AT BEST
MAKES LIFE FOR ME QUITE ROUGH.
WHAT HELPS ME GET THOUGH
IS KNOWING GOD'S GRACE AND MERCY IS ENOUGH.

YOU CAN'T HAVE JOYCE WITHOUT JOY

MY PURPOSE IS TO TELL YOU
WHAT JOY IS ALL ABOUT.

MY NAME AIN'T JOYCE FOR NOTHING
I BELIEVE THIS BEYOND A DOUBT.

THE STATE OF HAPPINESS IS
WHAT JOY SINCERELY MEANS.

EVERYONE WANTS JOY IT'S
VERY POPULAR IT SEEMS.

JOY ALSO IS SOMETHING WHERE
YOU CAN GET GREAT PLEASURE.

SATISFACTION IN ABUNDANCE SO
MUCH YOU'LL ALWAYS TREASURE.

COMPLETE HAPPINESS IS LIKE
PARADISE SOME CALL THIS BLISS.

THE STATUS IS SO DESIRED IF YOU
DON'T HAVE IT YOU WILL SURELY MISS.

JOY IS LIKE GRATUITY IT
GIVEN BEYOND WHAT'S DUE.

PLENTIFUL IS IN OCCURRENCE
AS IT'S FOR MORE THAN A FEW.

IT IS JUST LIKE CHRISTMAS WHEN
YOU GET YOUR FAVORITE TOY.

SO IT'S CERTAIN YOU CAN'T HAVE
JOYCE WITHOUT ALSO HAVING JOY!

SAFE ZONE VERSUS FAITH ZONE

MIRACLES DON'T HAPPEN WHEN
YOU STAY IN THE SAFE ZONE.

WHEN PETER STEPPED OUT ON THE WATER
IS ONE PLACE THIS IS SHOWN.

IF HE STAYED IN THE BOAT
HE WOULD HAVE NEVER KNEW.

THAT IF HE TRUSTED JESUS
WHAT THE LORD WOULD DO.

WHEN HIS FAITH GOT SHAKY
HE TOOK THE MASTER'S HAND.

THEN THE LORD LED HIM TO
A LESS THREATENING, SECURE LAND.

WHEN JESUS SAID COME
PETER DID HIS VERY BEST.

STRENGTH IS MADE COMPLETELY
PERFECT IN ANY WEAKNESS.

THERE ARE SOME RED SEAS GOD
WANTS TO PART FOR YOU.

BUT IF YOU STAY IN EGYPT YOU
WON'T SEE WHAT GOD WILL DO.

WHEN GOD FREES YOU FROM SOMETHING
HE'LL GET YOU TO THE NEXT PHASE.

THE LORD IS SO GOOD AT BEING GOD
HE'LL LEAVE YOU IN A DAZE.

GO AHEAD WALK ON THE WATER OR
WALK ON DRY LAND THROUGH THE SEAS.

THE LORD WILL TAKE CARE OF YOU
AND HE'LL NEVER LET YOU FREEZE.

MIRACLES DO HAPPEN WHEN YOU
STEP OUT IN THE FAITH ZONE.

WHEN PETER STEPPED OUT ON THE WATER
THIS IS ONE PLACE THIS WAS SHOWN.

SLAIN IN THE SPIRIT

SLAIN IN THE SPIRIT IS A TERM
THAT MANY DON'T UNDERSTAND.
I'M GOING TO EXPLAIN IT FOR
YOU THE BEST WAY THAT I CAN.

SURRENDERING ONES ENTIRE SELF TO
THE POWER OF THE HOLY GHOST.
WHEN THE SPIRIT COMES, THERE
IS NO WAY YOU CAN BOAST

THE SPIRIT MOVES IN DIFFERENT
WAYS ACCORDING TO WHO SUBMITS.
WHAT IT TAKES FOR OTHERS MAY BE
DIFFERENT WHEN IT'S YOU IT HITS.

THE SPIRIT MAKES SOME SHOUT AND
OTHERS MAY FALL TO THE FLOOR.
THE SPIRIT MAY EVEN MAKE SOME FOLKS
RUN RIGHT OUT OF THE CHURCH DOORS.

THE SPIRIT CHANGES MINDS AND
HEART AT ANY POINT IN TIME.
I'VE FELT IT MOVE IN ME QUITE OFTEN
AND IT'S AWESOME EVERYTIME.

THE MOVE OF THE SPIRIT ON ALL
FLESH WAS PROMISED IN THE BIBLE DAYS.
AND TODAY THE SPIRIT MOVES ALL
OVER TOUCHING HEARTS AND MENDING WAYS.

SOMEONE WHO LOVES ME

SOMEONE WHO LOVES ME
THAT REALLY DOESN'T HAVE TO.
SOMEONE WHO LOVES ME
WITH NO MOTIVE OR NO CLUE.

SOMEONE WHO LOVES ME
THAT WILL CAUSE ME NO HURT.
AND ALL HIS LOVE FOR ME
HE WILL NEVER DIVERT.

SOMEONE WHO LOVES ME
WHO LIGHTS UP AT THE SOUND OF MY VOICE.
SOMEONE WHO LOVES ME
SOLELY BY CHOICE.

SOMEONE WHO LOVES ME
THAT MELTS WHEN THEIR MIND FALLS ON ME.
SOMEONE WHO LOVES ME
WHOSE HEART I HOLD THE KEY.

SOMEONE WHO LOVES ME
WHO WAS MADE WITH ME IN MIND.
SOMEONE WHO LOVES ME
WHO WON'T REST UNTIL IT'S ME HE FINDS.

SOMEONE WHO LOVES ME
THAT ALWAYS LIGHTS MY FIRE.
SOMEONE WHO LOVES ME
WITH WHOM I CAN RETIRE.

SOMEONE WHO LOVES ME
THAT WILL ALWAYS BE AROUND.
SOMEONE WHO LOVES ME
AND OUR LOVE WILL MATCH POUND FOR POUND.

SOMEONE WHO LOVES ME
I CAN NO LONGER LIVE WITHOUT.
SOMEONE WHO LOVES ME
OF WHOM I HAVE NO DOUBT.

HE IS THE MISSING PIECE TO
MY PUZZLE AND I AM HIS
IF WE WERE A SODA
I AM THE SWEET HE IS THE FIZZ.

MY MAGNETIC FORCE WILL ATTRACT
HIM FAR GREATER THAN MOST.
WITH A POWER SO STRONG IT
WILL BE PRESENT ON ANY COAST.

HE WILL SATISFIED MY HUNGER
I KNOW THIS FOR A FACT.
MY THIRST WILL BE QUENCHED
AND THIS IS QUITE EXACT.

I JUST CAN'T WAIT TO
LAUGH AT HIS WIT.
IT REALLY WASN'T EASY
BUT I KNOW HE'S WORTH IT.

I KNOW I MUST HOLD ON
FOR AS LONG AS IT TAKES.
I NEED HIM READY FOR ME
I DON'T WANT HIM HALF BAKED.

I KNOW FOR CERTAIN
HE WILL COME FOR ME,
AS THE RIVER ALWAYS
FINDS THE SEA.

SOMEONE WHO LOVES ME
THAT WOULDN'T PLAY WITH MY HEART.
SOMEONE WHO LOVES ME
UNTIL DEATH DO WE PART.

SOMEONE WHO LOVES ME
AND BRING HAPPINESS I NEVER KNEW.
SOMEONE WHO LOVES ME
AND I'LL DO THE SAME FOR HIM, TOO.

SOMEONE WHO LOVES ME
LORD KNOWS HOW LONG I'VE WAITED.
SOMEONE WHO LOVES ME
AND FROM GOD WE HAVE BEEN MATED.

SOMEONE WHO LOVES ME
FROM SUNSET TO SUNRISE.
AND WHEN WE ARE TOGETHER
THE TIME ALWAYS JUST FLIES.

SOMEONE WHO LOVES ME
AND PREFER ME OVER ANY DESSERT.
AND TO DEFEND MY HONOR
HE WILL ALWAYS ASSERT.

THE MERE AROMA OF HIS
FAMILIAR MANLY SCENT
WILL LET ME KNOW FOR CERTAIN
THAT WE ARE TRULY MEANT.

SOMEONE WHO LOVES ME
THAT I WILL ENHANCE HIS LIFE.
SOMEONE WHO LOVES ME
AND HE WILL MAKE ME HIS WIFE.

SOMEONE WHO WILL LOVE ME
AND BRING THE WOMAN OUT OF ME.
SOMEONE WHO WILL COME SOON
JUST SIT BACK AND SEE!

SOMEONE WHO UNDERSTANDS ME
AND LOVES ME JUST THE SAME.
SOMEONE I WILL FOREVER CHERISH AND
WILL ALWAYS BEAR HIS NAME.

UNDERNEATH THE BLOOD

HOW DARE YOU GO UNDERNEATH THE BLOOD
TO PULL OUT SOMETHING IN MY PAST!
GOD HAS ALREADY FORGIVEN ME SO WHO ARE
YOU TO SAY HIS BLOOD WON'T LAST!

WHAT IS REALLY THE QUESTION HERE
MY SIN OR THE ABILITY OF THE SON?
DON'T YOU KNOW THE BATTLE HAS BEEN
FOUGHT AND THE VICTORY IS ALREADY WON!

THE SHEDDING OF HIS BLOOD IS
ABLE TO COVER A MULTITUDE OF SIN.
IT REALLY DOESN'T MATTER WHAT HAPPEN,
WHO DID IT, WHERE, OR WHEN.

THE FLOW OF BLOOD IS AVAILABLE
TO CLEANSE ALL SIN.
WE ALL MUST UTILIZE THIS FLOW AS
THIS IS THE ONLY WAY TO WIN.

SO YOU'VE GOT SOME NERVE TO GO UNDERNEATH
THE BLOOD TO GET SOMETHING FROM MY PAST!
MY GOD HAS FORGIVEN ME AND HIS BLOOD
IS SUFFICIENT ENOUGH TO LAST!

WHAT EVERY WOMAN SHOULD KNOW

EVERY WOMAN SHOULD KNOW
WHEN HER LIMIT IS REACHED.
EVERY WOMAN SHOULD KNOW
WHEN A LESSON IS BEING TEACHED.

EVERY WOMAN SHOULD KNOW
WHEN TO PACK UP HER GEAR.
EVERY WOMAN SHOULD KNOW
WHEN SHE DOES TO HAVE NO FEAR.

EVERY WOMAN SHOULD KNOW
HOW TO FALL IN LOVE WITHOUT BEING CONSUMED.
EVERY WOMAN SHOULD KNOW
WHEN A SITUATION IS DOOMED.

EVERY WOMAN SHOULD KNOW
HER TRUE CLOTHING SIZE.
EVERY WOMAN SHOULD KNOW
SHE SHOULD NEVER TELL LIES.

EVERY WOMAN SHOULD KNOW
WHO'S HER FRIEND RAIN OR SHINE.
EVERY WOMAN SHOULD KNOW
WHEN HER MATE COMES A GOOD THING HE'LL FIND.

EVERY WOMAN SHOULD KNOW
WHO TO LOVE AND WHOM TO TRUST.
EVERY WOMAN SHOULD KNOW
TO BE WHOLESOME AND JUST.

EVERY WOMAN SHOULD KNOW
HOW TO CARRY HER OWN WEIGHT.
EVERY WOMAN SHOULD KNOW
GOD IS THE AUTHOR AND FINISHER OF HER FATE.

EVERY WOMAN SHOULD KNOW
WHEN TO BE SWEET AND WHEN TO BE BOLD.
EVERY WOMAN SHOULD BE
PROUD OF HER AGE REGARDLESS TO HOW OLD.

EVERY WOMAN SHOULD KNOW
WHICH WAY TO GO AT THE FORK IN THE ROAD.
EVERY WOMAN SHOULD KNOW
GOD WILL HELP HER CARRY HER LOAD.

EVERY WOMAN SHOULD KNOW
WHEN TO BE NICE AND WHEN TO BE FIRM.
EVERY WOMAN SHOULD KNOW
NEVER TO COMPROMISE HER TERMS.

EVERY WOMAN SHOULD KNOW
THERE IS NO NEED TO CRY.
EVERY WOMAN SHOULD KNOW
FOR HER GOD SENT HIS ONLY SON TO DIE.

EVERY WOMAN SHOULD KNOW
SHE IS A DIAMOND IN THE ROUGH.
EVERY WOMAN SHOULD KNOW
THAT SHE IS SUPPOSED TO FEEL THAT MUSHY STUFF.

EVERY WOMAN SHOULD KNOW
SHE MUST STAND BY HER MAN.
EVERY WOMAN SHOULD KNOW
SHE MUST BE HIS NUMBER ONE FAN.

EVERY WOMAN SHOULD KNOW
ON HER GOD'S GOT HIS HAND.
EVERY WOMAN SHOULD KNOW
HE EVEN DROPS EVERY GRAIN OF SAND.

EVERY WOMAN SHOULD KNOW
HOW TO BE HUMBLE WHEN IT IS REQUIRED.
EVERY WOMAN SHOULD KNOW

THE DIFFERENCE BETWEEN BEING
UNHAPPY AND BEING TIRED.

EVERY WOMAN SHOULD KNOW
WHEN TO FORGIVE AND FORGET.
EVERY WOMAN SHOULD KNOW
THAT HER DATE WITH DESTINY IS SET.

EVERY WOMAN SHOULD KNOW
THERE IS NO NEED FOR DOUBT.
EVERY WOMAN SHOULD KNOW
IT'S NOT BECOMING TO POUT.

EVERY WOMAN SHOULD KNOW
SHE MUST LOVE HERSELF FIRST.
EVERY WOMAN SHOULD KNOW
IF SHE DOESN'T IT WILL ONLY MAKE THINGS WORSE.

EVERY WOMAN SHOULD KNOW
SHE GETS BETTER WITH TIME.
EVERY WOMAN SHOULD KNOW
WHEN THERE'S A MOUNTAIN HOW TO CLIMB.

EVERY WOMAN SHOULD KNOW
HOW TO WEATHER THE STORM.
EVERY WOMAN SHOULD KNOW
FROM GOD SHE WAS FORMED.

EVERY WOMAN SHOULD KNOW
HOW TO CARRY OUT HER DREAMS.
EVERY WOMAN SHOULD KNOW
THINGS AREN'T ALWAYS AS THEY SEEM.

EVERY WOMAN SHOULD KNOW
SHE SHOULD GIVE GOD ALL GLORY.
EVERY WOMAN SHOULD KNOW
SHE NEVER HAS TO WORRY.

EVERY WOMAN SHOULD KNOW
HOW TO FALL ON HER KNEES AND PRAY.
EVERY WOMAN SHOULD KNOW
WHEN SHE DOES TO KNOW JUST WHAT TO SAY.

EVERY WOMAN SHOULD KNOW
INTO A DIAMOND SHE'LL TURN.
ONCE SHE IS TRANSFORMED
AND ALL THE SHALLOWNESS IS BURNED

EVERY WOMAN SHOULD KNOW
THE ORGINIAL DIAMOND IS NOT ALL THAT AT FIRST.
IT HAS TO GO THROUGH SOMETHING
BEFORE IT'S TRUE IDENTITY IS BIRTHED

EVERY WOMAN SHOULD KNOW
NOT TO HAVE A CARE IN THE WORLD.
EVERY WOMAN SHOULD KNOW
SHE IS FOREVER DADDY'S PRECIOUS BABY GIRL!!!

DEDICATED TO

ALL MY CHILDHOOD FRIENDS

EVEN THE SCORE

ONE DAY I'M GOING TO LEARN
NOT TO DO THIS ANYMORE.
WHEN I DO MY HEART
WON'T HAVE TO BE THIS SORE.
I WILL NOT OPEN MYSELF UP,
TILT ME OVER, AND START TO POUR.
I MUST DEFEND MYSELF FROM
SATAN IN ORDER TO EVEN THE SCORE.

FOR I DON'T KNOW WHAT'S
BEST I CAN'T EVEN BE TRUSTED.
BECAUSE EVERTIME I THINK I CAN
MY HEART ENDS UP BUSTED.
SITTING ON THE FLOOR WITH MY BASKET EMPTY
AND ALL MY EGGS ARE CRACKED.
BECAUSE OF FILLING MY OWN VOID AGAIN
IN THE CORNER I AM BACKED.

THERE IS NO ONE ELSE TO BLAME
BUT ME, MYSELF, AND I.
IT HURTS SO BAD ALL
I WANT TO DO IS DIE.
I AM WALKING LIKE A DRUNK TAKING
ONE STEP FORWARD AND TWO BACK.
BY SATAN I'VE BEEN HELD AT GUNPOINT
AS THE YOUNG FOLK SAY I'VE DONE GOT JACKED.

THIS WALL I'VE BUILT AROUND ME
WHEN I LET IT DOWN IT'S ALL THE WAY.
I HAVE LEARNED BEFORE I DO THIS
I SHOULD GO TO GOD AND PRAY.
THIS ACTION WILL STOP UNJUST HURT
I REALLY DON'T HAVE TO FEEL.
TO PROTECT ME FROM ALL DANGER
AND KEEP ME IN GOD'S WILL.

TODAY I HAVE LEARNED
NOT TO DO THIS ANYMORE.
THIS WILL ASSURE ME THAT MY
HEART WILL NEVER BE THIS SORE.
WITHOUT GOD I WILL NOT OPEN MYSELF UP,
TILT MYSELF OVER, AND START TO POUR.
I WILL DEFEND MYSELF FROM SATAN IN
ORDER TO EVEN THE SCORE.

THIS TOO SHALL PASS

HOW CAN YOU SMILE WHILE YOUR HEART
IS BROKEN AND THROBBING WITH PAIN?
HOW CAN YOU LAUGH IN THE MIDST OF A
STORM WITHOUT SOMEWHAT FEELING INSANE?
HOW CAN YOU FEEL GOOD ABOUT YOURSELF
KNOWING WHAT YOU'VE DONE IN THE PAST?
YOU CAN DO THIS BECAUSE TO GOD
ALL YOUR BURDENS YOU CAN CAST.
OH YES, MY FRIEND, THIS TOO SHALL PASS!

WHEN YOU'VE SEARCH AND THERE
IS NOT A FRIEND TO BE FOUND.
WHEN YOU FEEL SO LOW YOU MUST
BE MILES BELOW THE GROUND.
WHEN YOU'VE BEAT YOURSELF SO BAD
BECAUSE OF ALL THE GUILT.
JUST REMEMBER GOD IS YOUR CREATOR
AND FROM HIS HANDS YOU WERE BUILT.
OH YES, MY FRIEND, THIS TOO SHALL PASS!

IF YOU'VE GIVEN IT YOUR ALL AND
YOU DON'T KNOW WHICH WAY TO TURN.
YOUR REACTION IS CRUCIAL BECAUSE
THERE IS A LESSON TO BE LEARNED.
DON'T WORRY ABOUT YOUR PAST.
DON'T WORRY ABOUT THE SHAME.
JESUS DIED FOR THIS ALREADY
AS THIS IS WHY HE CAME.
REST ASSURE, MY FRIEND, THIS TOO SHALL PASS!

WHEN YOU'VE CRIED ALL NIGHT LONG
AND YOU HAVE NO TEARS MORE TO CRY.
WHEN YOU HURT SO BAD YOU WANT
TO JUST CURL UP AND DIE.
THAT IS NOT THE ANSWER,
NO, THAT IS NOT THE KEY.

CALL ON JESUS FOR HELP CAUSE AT HIS
NAME THE DEMONS HAVE TO FLEE.
WITH CALM CERTAINTY, MY FRIEND,
THIS TOO SHALL PASS!

IF ONLY

IF ONLY I COULD SEE
YOUR FACE JUST ONCE MORE.
IF ONLY WE COULD SIT ON THE
PORCH JUST LIKE WE DID BEFORE.
DADDY, I WISH YOU WOULD HOLD MY
HAND LIKE WHEN WE WALKED TO THE STORE.
I WISH I COULD STARE UP AT YOU
AS I SAT DOWN ON THE FLOOR.
THE TWINKLE IN YOUR BIG BROWN EYES
TOLD ME WHAT YOU FELT FOR ME.
IT CHANGED THE COLDNESS OF THE
WORLD TO WARMTH AND SECURITY.

IF ONLY YOUR BIG STRONG ARMS WOULD
HOLD ME JUST ONCE MORE.
IF ONLY I COULD SEE YOU WALK UP ON THE
PORCH AND COME RIGHT IN THE DOOR.
I WISH I COULD GO BACK IN TIME TO HUG
YOUR NECK AND KISS YOUR CHEEK.
THEN MAYBE YOU COULD COME FORWARD
IN MY LIFE TO TAKE A PEEK.
ALTHOUGH OUR TIME TOGETHER IN THE FLESH
HAD TO COME TO AN END.
THE LOVE YOU GAVE ME WILL STAY
WITH ME ON THAT I CAN DEPEND.

FOR MY TO WHOM

YOU SEE, WE LIVED IN THE SAME WOMB.
WE PROBABLY ATE OFF THE SAME SPOON.
WE ALSO SLEPT IN THE SAME ROOM.
TOGETHERNESS FROM MIDNIGHT UNTIL NOON.
WE KNOW WE ENJOYED THE SAME BOOM.
WE EVEN DANCED TO THE SAME TUNES.
MANY TIMES WE SHARED IN THE SAME GLOOM.
WE GREW UP THEN ROSE FROM OUR COCOONS
OUR SEPARATE WAYS WE WENT ZOOM, ZOOM.
WHY DID OUR BOND BECOME SO DOOMED?
HOW DID WE GET TO THST PLACE OF LOOM?
YET, WE STILL CRIED AT THE SAME TOMBS.
WE VOWED TO MAKE IT RIGHT REALLY SOON.
WE HAD TO JUST TAKE OFF THE COSTUMES.
SO THERE WAS NOTHING LEFT TO ASSUME.
OUR HEARTS STILL LOVED US TO THE MOON.
THIS LOVE IS AS SWEET AS PERFUME.
THIS IS WHAT WE DID FOR OUR TO WHOM.

DEPEND ON AND TRUST

YOU ARE THE ONLY ONE I CAN DEPEND ON AND TRUST.
YOUR LEAD IS MY GUIDE IN LIFE AND IS TRULY A MUST.
I NEED YOU IN ALL THINGS; I AM NOT AFRAID TO TELL.
YOU ARE AWESOME, AMAZING AND YOU'LL NEVER FAIL.
I MAY NOT UNDERSTAND THE ROUTE YOU SAY TO GO.
AFTER ALL IS MANIFEST, THE PROOF IS IN THE SHOW.
WHEN I MESS UP USING ONLY MY OWN CHORE.
YOUR PROMPTING LEADS ME BACK
AND THIS I DO ADORE.
YOU ARE THE ONE I CAN DEPEND ON AND TRUST.
YOU ARE THE BEST AND MORE THAN A HUGE PLUS.

COMMITMENT

STRIVING EVERYDAY TO BRING MY
ACTIONS UNDER SUBJECTION.
FOR WHEN I SEARCH FOR ME I RECOGNIZE
MY OWN REFLECTION.
MADE IN GOD'S OWN IMAGE MY DEEDS
SHOULD LOOK THE SAME.
I REPRESENT THE LORD AND SAVIOR;
I'M LIFTING UP HIS HOLY NAME.
I DO ELECT TO FOLLOW THE ROAD THAT
IS STRAIGHT AND NARROW.
LORD, I KNOW YOU WATCH ME AS
YOUR EYE IS ON THE SPARROW.
MASTER, I BELIEVE YOU WROTE THE
WAY MY FUTURE WILL UNFOLD.
I KNOW AND LOOK FORWARD TO WHEN
YOUR FACE I WILL BEHOLD.
IN THE MEANTIME, THIS MARATHON OF
LIFE I WILL CONTINUE TO RUN.
UNTIL THE TIME WHEN YOU SAY MY
WORK HERE ON EARTH IS DONE.

HUMBLE PRAYER

LORD, I COME TO YOU THIS DAY AS
HUMBLY AS I KNOW HOW.
THANKING YOU FOR YOUR LOVE AND
MY HEAD TO YOU I BOW.

I AM GRACIOUS TO YOU FOR THE BLESSING;
I HAVEN'T ROOM TO RECEIVE.
I HONOR YOU FOR YOUR SACRIFICE; IN
YOU I WILL ALWAYS BELIEVE.

FOR THAT WHICH WAS ON CALVARY, I
AM GRATEFUL IT IS NO MORE.
I HAVE ACCEPTED YOU AS MY SAVIOR; I
WALKED RIGHT IN THAT DOOR.

EVEN IN MY HUMAN STATE, YOU ARE
WITH ME RIGHT BY MY SIDE.
NEVER WILL YOU FORSAKE ME AS THIS
IS WHY YOU ROSE AND DIED.

KEEP YOUR HANDS UPON ME AS I
DESIRE TO ALWAYS DO MY PART.
I LOVE YOU DEEPLY WITH MY MIND,
SOUL, AND ALL OF MY HEART.

I ASK THIS ALL IN JESUS' NAME AND ALSO FOR HIS SAKE.
TO HONOR YOU AND ALL MY CARES
TO YOU I WILL TAKE. AMEN!

JESUS' RIGHTEOUSNESS

NOT EVEN THE VERY BEST ONE HAS
ANY REAL HOLINESS TO SPEAK.
NOT EVEN WHEN WE ARE MOST UPRIGHT
AND WITH GOODNESS AT ITS PEAK.

DO YOU THINK YOU ARE AS GOOD AS JESUS
AND FEEL HIS ETERNAL LIFE YOU DESERVE?
IF YOU DO, I AM SORRY AND MUST TELL YOU
GOD DOES NOT GRADE ON A CURVE.

YOU CANNOT GET TO HEAVEN BY YOUR OWN
RIGHTEOUSNESS OR YOUR WELL WORKS.
THESE DEEDS ARE DONE AS GRATITUDE FOR
BEING ABLE TO BECOME GOD'S CONVERT.

THE BIBLE SAYS WE ALL HAVE SINNED. THERE
IS NOT A PERSON WORTHY, NOT EVEN ONE
JESUS IS THE ONLY MAN WHO LIVED A LIFE
WITHOUT SIN; YES, JESUS GOD'S ONLY SON.

WE ARE ALL IN DIER NEED OF THE SAVIOR
AND I PRAY YOU ACCEPT THIS FATE.
JESUS EXCLUSIVELY CAN FORGIVE US
AND WIPE CLEAN ALL OUR SLATE.

WE MUST ABANDON ALL HOPE OF OUR
GOODNESS PLAYING A PART IN ANY WAY.
TO KNOW THAT JESUS DID IT ALL HIS DEATH
AND WHEN HE ROSE ON THE THIRD DAY.

ETERNAL LIFE BEGINS WITH OUR FAITH AND BELIEF
IN THE LORD; AND NOT WITH OUR DEATH.
IT IS AN EARTHLY DEPOSIT THAT ALLOWS US TO
KNOW WE HAVE COME INTO OUR WEALTH.

JESUS PAID THE DEBT WE INCURRED FROM
BEING BORN IN AND COMMITTING SIN.
SO, BY FAITH HE GAVE US RIGHTEOUSNESS TO
OFFER US THE LORD IN ORDER TO WIN.

NEXT TIME SOMEONE ASKS YOU, "IS
HEAVEN YOUR ETERNAL HOME?"
REPLY "YES" AND THE STREETS OF GOLD
IS WHERE YOU WILL ROAM.

LEFT FOR DEAD

THE ENEMY LEFT YOU FOR DEAD;
YET, YOU ARE STILL ALIVE.
YOU WILL RECOVER FROM THIS MISHAP
ONLY AGAIN TO THRIVE.

HE WROTE YOUR OBITUARY BECAUSE
HE THOUGHT YOU WERE DONE.
THE VICTORY BELONGS TO GOD; SATAN
SURELY CAN'T HAVE NONE.

LEFT FOR DEAD BUT ONLY
GOD HAS THE SAY ON THAT.
ON THE THRONE OF GLORY
IS WHERE HE'S ALWAYS SAT.

SATAN COUNTED YOU OUT AND SAID
THAT YOU WERE FINISHED
WITH GOD ON YOUR SIDE THAT
STING IS SOON DIMINISHED.

THE ASSIGNMENT TO KILL IN THE
MIND OF SATAN WAS HATCHED.
YOU ARE IN THE MASTER'S HAND AND
YOU CANNOT BE SNATCHED.

HE THOUGHT HE HAD YOU DOWN; HE
THOUGHT HE HAD YOU OUT.
GOD STEPPED IN AND THE ENEMY'S HEAD
IS WHERE YOUR FOOT IS MOUNT.

SATAN SETS SNARES THAT CERTAINLY WILL NOT SUCCEED
GOD MADE SURE IT DIDN'T PROSPER;
YES, HE DID INDEED.

THE LORD IS BIGGER THAN
ANYTHING SATAN CAN PREPARE.

I DON'T UNDERSTAND WHY
HE ATTEMPTS TO DARE.

AGAINST ALL ODDS
I CANNOT EXPLAIN.
SATAN'S LOSS IS TRULY
HEAVEN'S GAIN.

GROWTH IN THE STRUGGLE

I REMEMBER LONG AGO WHEN I WAS A LITTLE GIRL.
ADORNED IN LACE, PATENT LEATHER, AND LONG CURLS.

SINGING TO MY DOLLS ABOUT
ANCIENT SWEET, LULLABIES.
IS WHEN MY MOMMY TOLD ME A
STORY ABOUT BUTTERFLIES.

THERE IS GOOD NEWS WITH AN UNDERLYING MESSAGE.
PAY CLOSE ATTENTION AND YOU WILL CATCH IT.

THE STRUGGLE BEING PORTRAYED
IS MOST DEFINITELY REAL.
AS THERE IS ESSENTIAL KNOWLEDGE
HIDDEN IN THE DEAL.

MOMMY TOLD ME THE BUTTERFLY
BEGAN AS A CATERPILLAR.
IF FORMED A COCOON THAT COVERED
IT LIKE A CASE OF A BED PILLOW.

WHILE INSIDE THE COCOON IT STRUGGLED,
STRETCHED, AND FOUGHT.
WITH GREAT FORCE AND MIGHT THE
BUTTERFLY WAS BEING TAUGHT.

THIS ACTIVITY CONTINUED UNTIL THE
DAY IT CAME BURSTING OUT.
THIS WAS THE RIGHT WAY; YES, THIS
WAS ALSO THE RIGHT ROUTE.

IF BUTTERFLIES DIDN'T STRUGGLE, THEY
WOULD NEVER LEARN TO FLY.
IT WOULD CRAWL AROUND ON THE
GROUND AND EVENTUALLY DIE.

ITS PURPOSE WOULD BE VOID
IN OTHER WORDS UTTERLY DESTROYED.

AS IT NEVER GAINED THE POWER
TO FLY AS PURPOSED IN ITS SAID HOUR.

YOUR COCOON'S PURPOSE IS GRAND.
IT IS A PART OF GOD'S PLAN.

TO GIVE YOU ENDURANCE FOR THIS RACE.
TO GET YOU TO YOUR RIGHTFUL PLACE.

DON'T FUSS ABOUT THE STRUGGLE;
DON'T CRY ABOUT THE FIGHT.
FOR THIS WILL GIVE YOU POWER TO
MAKE IT DURING LIFE'S FLIGHT.

GOD'S WARNING

DON'T CHOOSE TO IGNORE THIS BECAUSE
IT MIGHT BE YOUR LAST TIME.
ALL YOUR LIFE, I HAVE BEEN KNOCKING
IN ME SALVATION YOU'LL FIND.

SEEK ME NOW WHILE I AM AVAILABLE
AND LONGING TO BE FOUND.
IF YOU DON'T AND WAIT TOO LATE
YOU WILL BE HELL BOUND.

EVERYWHERE YOU HAVE GONE; I
WENT ALONG FOR THE RIDE.
IN HOPES THAT WHEN YOU GOT WEARY
IN MY ARMS YOU WOULD SLIDE.

YOU DECIDED TO TAKE A CHANCE AND WAIT
TO SEEK ME WITH YOUR LAST BREATH.
UNFORTUNATELY, WHEN THE TIME CAME
YOU LOOKED UP AND THERE WAS DEATH.

WITHOUT A CHANCE TO SCREAM OR HOLLER
NOT EVEN A CHANCE TO REPENT.
NOW, YOUR ETERNITY IS CERTAIN AND
HELL IS WHERE YOURS WILL BE SPENT.

OH, MY FRIEND DON'T LET THIS HAPPEN.
WAKE UP THIS WAS JUST A DREAM.
IT CAME STRAIGHT FROM GOD AS HE IS
THE ONE AND ONLY SUPREME.

WARNING ALWAYS COME BEFORE
DESTRUCTION; THIS IS WHAT I'M TOLD.
ACCEPT GOD AS YOUR SAVIOR AND
DON'T LET THIS DREAM UNFOLD.

AFTERTHOUGHT I

Now granted I am the baby girl, in fact I am the only girl in my family. I was the only one of my parent's children to attend private school. All of my needs were met. I can't recall wanting for anything. Each of my immediate family members always made sacrifices to make sure everything I needed and wanted was supplied. All of this I would have given up in an instant if only I could have had both my parents, at least until my eighteenth birthday. To be honest I very often felt cheated. All my brothers had both parents at least that long. I could not figure out what I had done to deserve this horrible event, the death of my father, at such an early age.

Now, of course you know that only Satan would stoop as low as to making an eleven-year old child think that their father's death was her fault or the result of something she had done. Satan wanted this event to scare me for the rest of my life. He wanted my father's death to push me away from GOD, but on the contrary GOD had something else in mind. No matter how things look, GOD has our best interest at hand. The death of my natural father taught me to lean solely on GOD the Father.

My daddy made certain that all of his children knew the twenty-third Psalm. Looking back now I know why. The revelation has come and now I know how I made it through the most painful experience in my life! "Yea thou I walk through the valley of the shadow of death I will fear no evil. Thy rod and thy staff they comfort me. Thou prepareth a table before me in the presence of mine enemies. Thou anointed my head with oil. My cup runneth over. Surely goodness and mercy shall follow me all the days of my life and I will dwell in the house of the LORD forever."

Yes, Satan I am going to fully expose you for what you are today. Even suicidal thoughts torment me on many occasions during some of my down periods. These thoughts are to the extent of receiving exact instructions from Satan on how to end the pain. One incident that comes to mind is a period during my cycle as a single parent. I had grown extremely depressed and frustrated with my life. Satan told me to go and get a razor from the bathroom and slit my wrist. He didn't tell me to slit it in the usual manner, but to cut it in a horizontal manner to be certain of my demise. I recall praying and asking GOD to intervene. GOD did just that. My children were in their room and all of a sudden they required my immediate attention. I went to them and attended to their needs. This took my attention off Satan's attack against me. After I finished with the children the effect of Satan's tactic against me lost its stronghold on me. At that point a revelation from GOD came to me that I was focusing too much on what Satan was telling me, and I was giving him the power over me. I was told that I must rebuke him and take the power I had given him back. From that day until this day, Satan has not attacked me again in the form of suicide. Apparently Satan took me to be a fool, but he's the fool, not me. For my GOD loves me too much for me to listen to that mess Satan was trying to tell me. I'm daddy's baby girl and I'll never forget it. And you, too, should feel the same way.

AFTERTHOUGHT II

The result of some circumstance effect everyone involved differently. If the circumstance is death, birth, divorce, marriage or some other tragedy, it affects everyone either directly or indirectly. For instance, the death of very good friend's mother totally devastated my dear friend. His mother means the world to him and there is nothing he would not do to bring her back. My friend is a very strong man in wisdom, experience and statute. He and I have been friends for nine plus years and I have never known him to cry for any reason except during the time his mother became ill and passed. This man fought in the Vietnam War and his life was at stake every moment possible, he witnessed killing and death on a daily basis, he experienced many tragedies throughout his life and never allowed one tear to fall from his eyes. Yet after enduring all these things in life this same man has such a loving, trusting, genuine, tenderness for his mother as though he were a newborn child.

On me, however, his mother's death has had a completely different effect. It has allowed me to look at my own mother in a way that is very odd to me. I can't imagine my mother not being with me. I don't think that my mother will ever die or is it that I just won't allow myself to accept this possibility because I'm not ready. My friend's mother's death also reminded me of how precious the time is that I spend with my mother. It allowed me to become aware of the fact that the last time we see someone may in fact be, at that instance, the final time we see them. Because of this I give extra attention to my mother and I try to make sure that the time we spend together is a time of quality and substance. Now more than ever I savor the time I spend with my mother.

I discussed the death of my friend's mother with my mother. I am sure this situation affected her in a different way from the way it affected me, because as I discussed the situation with my mother, I could hear the great compassion and wisdom in her voice. Why? Because she, too, has lost her mother. My mother spoke with my friend and she told him she could understand exactly how he felt. She told him to look at this situation from all angles. She reminded him that he did not want his mother to suffer and that her memory would always dwell within him. She went on to tell him that, one day, if he accepted JESUS CHRIST as his LORD and Savior and live right that he would indeed be with her in eternity. My mother got a chance to use her experience to help my friend in his time of need. She passed along to him what she learned from her experience to give him comfort and this is what we are supposed to do.

AFTERTHOUGHT II

CONTINUATION

When the time comes my friend will pass along the same information to someone else. For my mother this situation brought back memories of her own mother and the legacy she left behind.

The death of my friend's mother affected my children in yet another way. They began to realize (not that they hadn't before), that no one lives forever and that death comes to all. They started inquiring about what happens after physical death. Believe me, questions were coming from every angle. I explained to them that their soul is the only thing that they have legitimate claims on forever. I also explained to them the process of life in the body and I told them that some day their body would grow old and die. But, their soul, that is inside will separate from their physical makeup and live on forever. I reminded them that their soul was what was inside of them; it knows wrong from right and it sometimes hurts and at other times feels joy. I let them know that it was very important that they make the conscious decision while in the body where their eternity would be spent. I made them fully aware that hell is real and filled with pain, sorrow, and suffering. I stressed that I did not want them to spend their eternity in hell, but I had no control over that. Finally, I told them that heaven is real and this is the place to go because there is nothing but love, joy, peace, and happiness in heaven! Heaven is a place where you will never hurt again. GOD wants all of his children to go to heaven. He gave us all the same opportunity to achieve this goal. But we all must make this decision prior to death and neither of us knows where death lies.

All these feelings and reactions came from one incident. The number of people this situation affected and their reactions is unknown. This situation has certainly, however, touched and moved many. Everyone's actions effect many people directly or indirectly. Life is a whirlwind of circumstances. Our reactions and feelings about each situation define our character.

WHEN MOMMA LEFT . . .

This woman must say she has seen her share of heartache, pain, and disappointment. She has been known to say one day she might start to cry and she will have no tears left to flow because she has used all her share. At one of her lowest times was surrounding her mother's death. You see she and her mom had a special relationship. The way her mom would introduced her to people was priceless. She would always says in a way only she could do; "This is my one and only daughter, and yes she my baby too." This always made Joyce smile every time. Now the time had come where her mom had to leave her earthen vessel. This lady held her mother's hand until she died and some time afterward, too. She was tore up inside but she knew there was no time for grieving. She knew she had to fulfill all of her mother's wishes in dignity and with a clear mind. She knew it was her duty as she was her mother's only daughter. She held it all together; she dotted every "i" and crossed every "t". She took care of ever detail no matter how minute. After the funeral she knew next she had to make sure the headstone was ordered then laid. While she was waiting for the headstone, she didn't know whether to turn off the utilities at her mom's house. She left the utilities on. The headstone was in place four months after the funeral; She exhaled. Five more months passed before she turned the utilities off at her mom's house. At that point she lost it. She could not believe she had not heard her momma's voice in nine months. Later, she realize she hadn't accepted her mother's death until she turned the utilities off at her mom's house and that was the beginning of her grieving process. She could barely eat (one Vienna sausage & ½ cup of vanilla pudding per day) and her body was literally shaking most of the time. She was always crying. She lost thirty pounds in two weeks. She could not pray. She didn't know what to pray. She got to the place where she was afraid to leave her house. Later she learned the condition of being afraid to leave her home was called agoraphobia. She would call on the name of Jesus day in and day out. She was so bad off she asked her family to take her to a mental facility. They said no.

In all this disparity, God showed His sense of humor. One afternoon a few weeks later she decided to try to take the trash out through the garage to the garbage barrel in the yard and she got locked out of her house. Therefore, she had to sit outside until someone came home to let her back her house. God got her out of the house! Before this happened, she had asked certain people to pray for her and by the Grace of God about three weeks later she was feeling better and able to pray for herself again. God got all the glory. Praise His Holy Name!

ABOUT THE AUTHOR

The late Reverend David Richard and his wife Evelyn Wingate Richard desired to have a daughter named "Joyce" ever since they married in June of 1948. Finally, seventeen years and four pregnancies later on February 11, 1965 Joyce Ionna Richard was born. Joyce is the youngest of a family of four children and the only princess, I mean girl. Being the youngest and the only female proved to be very beneficial for Joyce growing up, and she discovered this at an early age. Joyce was a very happy and spoiled child. As a child she knew of some of the gifts that GOD had given to her, but she didn't discover the extent of these gifts until many, many, years later.

On January 2, 1977 Joyce was devastated. She and her brother Philip found their father lying on the front yard. The Reverend David Richard, Joyce's father, had suffered from a heart attack. Months before this happened a depression had settled on Joyce and she knew something awful was going to happen. She started asking a lot of "What If" questions during this period, and when she saw her father lying there that cold and rainy night she knew deep inside that this was what she was dreading and she knew her father was going to die. After the ambulance took him away Joyce told her grandmother that she knew her daddy would never come back home. Joyce's father died a few days later on January 5, 1977 in spite of his appearing to get better.

Joyce now knows that the period following her father's death she suffered a nervous breakdown at the age of eleven. She also knows that only GOD's grace brought her through. During this time, a time of complete despair Joyce wrote her first poem ever. Joyce quickly came to realize that writing poetry was the only positive way she could express her feelings and emotions. Joyce was diagnosed with Lupus in 1983. She suffered with bouts of this disease through 1998. New Year's day 1999 Joyce asked GOD for a complete healing from Lupus and she has been Lupus-free every since. At age twenty, Joyce married, and in spite of numerous doctors reports that she would probably never have children she was blessed with four beautiful children, Ta Shara Baldwin, Dwight Baldwin, Jr., Nickolas Baldwin, and Destiny Montgomery. Joyce considers her children the most precious gift a mother could ask for and she often says, "My children are my best asset." Joyce's first three children are all approximately sixteen months apart. Joyce has a brief chapter in her life as being an unwed pregnant teenager/mother as her first child was born when she was one month shy of her being 20 years old. Yes, this was prior to her first marriage; although her first three children have the same father, her ex husband. Destiny's father is her second and current husband.

When Joyce divorced her first husband, it began another chapter in her life as a single parent. Joyce was on her own with an eight, seven and six year old. Again deep emotions triggered Joyce to write poetry. Now more than ever Joyce realized that the wonderful gift of writing poetry would allow others to draw pictures in their minds of the words she had written. With GOD as the dictator and Joyce as the writer Joyce began writing a series of poems to help and encourage others in times of distress. On and off for the next three years Joyce wrote poetry. She complied each into the book you are holding in your hands right now. Also, during the midst of this three years GOD called Joyce to preach the gospel.

On February 17, 2002 at four o'clock p.m. Joyce Richard Montgomery preached her initial sermon. In a well-attended audience at The Restoration International Praise and Worship Center under the leadership of Reverend Leon Rankins, III, Joyce had her first real date with destiny. It is Joyce's prayer that the readers will be blessed by at least one of these poems if not all of them. It is also her heart's desire that souls will be saved, people will be delivered and set free by reading this book.

In conclusion, Ms. Montgomery has done her part in allowing GOD to use her every step of the way. Now it is up to GOD and you, the readers, to do the rest. May GOD forever bless and keep all of his children is Ms. Montgomery's final prayer.

Daddy's Baby Girl Forever Ministries
montgomery_joyce@rocketmail.com

ORIGINAL KINGDOM PATRONS

EVELYN W. RICHARD
HAZEL W. LYMAN
EOLA M. MOORE
ROHAVEN RICHARD
JOHN D. RICHARD
WILLIE FRED RICHARD
ELLA MAE RICHARD DAVIS
REV. AND MINISTER DARROLD AND
KAREN MONTGOMERY
MR. AND MRS. DAVID AND ANN RICHARD
MR. AND MRS. PHILIP AND ESTHER RICHARD
MR. AND MRS. GERALD AND GRACIE RICHARD
PATRICIA WATTS
TIMOTHY BOOKER
ROBIN PEAGLER
CHERYL LOVELACE
DELORES ALLEN MC CAULEY
MR. AND MRS. VALEN AND JANICE WARREN
MR. AND MRS. LEE AND DELLA ABBOTT
MINISTER KIERON COLE
MINISTER O'NEAL MCRUNNELLS
REV. AND MINISTER LEON AND MELBA RANKINS
REV. AND MRS. ZEBEDEE NICHOLSON
MR. AND MRS. EDDIE AND CONNIE ALLEN
DR. CLAYTON COLEMAN
EDNA RANKINS
MR. AND MRS. LAMONT AND MARJORIE MCPIKE
CORRIE O. WINGATE
CARRIE DEBERRY
MR. AND MINISTER ANTHONY AND CARMEN WILSON
FLORENCE PITTS
SANDRA WHITING
WILLIE MAE RANDERSON
DEACON RICHMOND WILLIAMS
ARTIS STROMAS
ARISTINE SHEPPARD

ANDREA FLOYD
MR AND MRS LORENZO AND ETHEL EVANS
MR. AND MRS. DERRICK AND LANISKA LEATHERWOOD
MR. AND MINSTER ALPHONZE AND JOYCE ARNOLD
GWENDOLYN (COOKIE) SPIVEY
MARY DOBBINS
MR. AND MRS. NEIL AND MARY CARTER
SANDRA HADLEY
DEBORAH PRIM
MINISTER CASSANDRA JOHNSON GREEN
MRS. VARZELL CARTER
FAYE NICHOLS
LOIS BOYKINS
ODESSA HILL LEON RANKINS, JR

MUCH THANKS AND MANY BLESSINGS!
I LOVE EACH OF YOU WITH MY WHOLE HEART!

JOYCE

SCRIPTURES FOOD FOR THE SOUL, MIND, BODY, AND SPIRIT

For as he thinks in his heart so is he. Proverbs 23:7

GOD'S love has been poured out in our hearts through the HOLY SPIRIT who has been given to us. Romans 5:5

For GOD so loved the world that HE gave HIS one and only son that whoever believes in HIM shall not perish, but have eternal life. John 3:16

If you confess with you mouth, "JESUS IS LORD," and believe in your heart that GOD raised JESUS from the dead, you will be saved. Romans 10:9

But GOD chose the foolish things of the world to shame the wise, GOD chose the weak things of the world to shame the strong. He chose the lowly things of this world, the despised things, and the things that are not-to nullify the things that are, so that no one may boost before him . . . therefore, as it is written: "Let him who boasts boast in the LORD. 1st Corinthians 1:27-31

Do you know that in a race all the runners run, but only one gets the prize? Run in such a way as to get the prize. Everyone who competes in the game goes into strict training. They do it to get a crown that will not last; but we do it to get a crown that will last forever. 1st Corinthians 9:24 and 25

Now the LORD is the SPIRIT and where the SPIRIT of the LORD is, there is freedom. And we, who with unveiled faces all reflect the LORD'S GLORY which comes from the LORD who is the SPIRIT. 2nd 3:17 and 18 Corinthians

But thanks be to GOD, who always leads us in triumphal procession in CHRIST and through us spread everywhere the fragrance of the knowledge of him. For we are to GOD, the aroma of CHRIST, among those who are being saved and those who are perishing. 2nd Corinthians 2:14 and 15

As GOD'S fellow workers we urge you not to receive GOD'S GRACE in vain. For he says, in the time of my favor I heard you, and in the day of SALVATION I helped you. I tell you, now is the time of GOD'S FAVOR, now is the day of SALVATION. 2nd Corinthians 6:1 and 2

I am not ashamed of the GOSPEL, because it is the power of GOD for the SALVATION of everyone who believes . . . for in the GOSPEL a righteousness from GOD is revealed a righteousness that is by faith from first to last, just as it is written: "The righteous will live by faith. Romans 1:16 and 17

The mind of a sinful man is death, but the mind controlled by the spirit is life and peace. Romans 8:6

And we know that in all things GOD works for the good of those who love HIM, who have been called according to HIS purpose. Romans 8:28

I will look on you with favor and make you fruitful and increase your numbers, and I will keep my covenant with you. You will be still eating last year's harvest when you will have to move it out to make room for the new. Leviticus 26:9 and 10

No, in all these things we are more than conquerors through him who loved us. For I am convinced that neither death nor life, neither angels nor demons, neither the present, nor the future, nor any powers, neither heights, nor depths, nor anything else in all creations will be able to separate us from the love of GOD that is in CHRIST JESUS our LORD. Romans 8:37-39

Therefore, I urge you brothers, in view of GOD'S MERCY, to offer your bodies as living sacrifices HOLY and pleasing to GOD-this is your spiritual act of worship. Do not conform any longer to the pattern of this world, but be transformed by the renewing of your mind. Then you will be able to test and approve what GOD'S WILL is-HIS good, pleasing, and perfect WILL. Romans 1:1 and 2

For we will all stand before GOD'S judgment seat. It is written: "As surely as I live, says the LORD, every knee will bow before me: every tongue will confess to GOD." So then, each of us will give an account of himself to GOD. Romans 14:9-11

May the GOD of hope fill you with all joy and peace as you trust in him, so that you may overflow with hope by the power of the HOLY SPIRIT. Romans 15:13

For we are GOD'S workmanship, created in CHRIST JESUS to do good works, which GOD prepared in advance for us to do. Ephesians 2:10

And in him you too are being built together to become a dwelling in which GOD lives by his SPIRIT. Ephesians 2:22

Finally, be strong in the LORD and in HIS mighty power. Put on the full armor of GOD so that you can take your stand against the devil's schemes. For our struggle is not against flesh and blood, but against the rulers, against the authorities, against the powers of this dark world and against the spiritual forces of evil in the HEAVENLY REALMS. Ephesians 6:10-12

Endure hardship as discipline; GOD is treating you as sons. For what son is not disciplined by his father? Hebrews 12:7

You need to persevere as that when you have done the will of GOD, you will receive what he has promised. Hebrews 10:36

I can do everything through him who gives me strength. Philippians 4:13

Let us then approach the throne of GRACE with confidence, so that we may receive MERCY and find GRACE to help us in our time of need. Hebrews 4:16

Let us not become weary in doing good, for at the proper time we will reap a harvest if we do not give up. Galatians 6:9

Love your neighbor as yourself. Galatians 5:14

It is not for you to know the times or dates the father has set by his authority, but you will receive the power when the HOLY SPIRIT comes on you. Acts 1:7 and 8

. . . I have set before you life and death, blessings and curses. Now choose life, so that you and your children may live and that you may love the LORD your GOD, listen to his voice, and hold fast to him. For the LORD is your life, and he will give you many years in the land he swore to give to your fathers, Abraham, Isaac, and Jacob. Deuteronomy 30:19-20

For in him we live, move, and have our being. Act 17:28

However, I consider my life worth nothing to me: if only I may finish the task for testifying to the gospel of GOD'S GRACE. Acts 20:24

For I know the plans I have for you, declares the LORD, "plans to prosper you and not to harm you, plans to give you hope and a future. Then you will call upon me, come, and pray to me and I will listen to you. You will seek me and find me when you seek me with all your heart. Jeremiah 29:11-13

Cursed is the one who trust in man, who depends on flesh for his strength and whose heart turns away from the LORD. But blessed is the man who trusts in the LORD whose confidence is in him. Jeremiah 17:5 and 7

Forget the former things do not dwell on the past. See I am doing a new thing. I am making a way in the desert and streams in the wasteland. The wild animals honor me, the jackals and the owls, because I provided water in the desert and streams in the wasteland to give drink to my people. My chosen, the people I formed for myself that they may proclaim my praise. Isaiah 43:18-21

But those who hope in the LORD will renew their strengths. They will soar on wings like eagles; they will run and not grow weary they will walk and not be faint. Isaiah 40:31

Train yourself to be GODLY. 1st Timothy 4:7

Bear with each other and forgive whatever grievances you may have against one another. Forgive as the LORD forgave you. Colossians 3:13

A man can receive only what is given him from HEAVEN. John 3:27

So, if the son set you free, you will be free indeed. John 8:36

I tell you the truth my father will give you whatever you ask in my name. Ask and you will receive, and your joy will be complete. John 16:23 and 24

With authority and power he gives orders to evil spirits and they come out! Luke 4:36

When an evil spirit comes out of a man, it goes through arid places seeking rest and does not find it. Then it says, "I will return to the house I left." When it arrives, it finds the house unoccupied, swept clean and put in order. Then it goes and takes with it seven other spirits more wicked than itself and they go in and live there. And the final condition of that man is worse than the first. That is how it will be with this wicked generation. Matthew 12:43-45

"With man this is impossible, but with GOD all things are possible." Matthew 19:26

Everything is possible for him who believes. Mark 9:23

Consider it pure joy, my brothers, whenever you face trials of many kinds, because you know that the testing of your faith develops perseverance. Perseverance must finish its work so that you may be mature and complete not lacking anything. James 1:2-4

Because of the LORD'S great love we are not consumed, for his compassions never fail. They are new every morning: Great is your faithfulness. I say to myself, "The LORD is my portion, therefore, I will wait for him. Lamentations 3:22-24

A sinner's wealth is stored up for the righteous. Proverbs 13:22

For a man's way are in full view of the LORD. Proverbs 3:5

Trust in the LORD with all your heart and lean not on your own understanding; in all your ways acknowledge HIM and HE will make your paths straight. Proverb 15:32

A wise man's heart guides his mouth and his lips promote instruction. Proverbs 16:23

The LORD detest the sacrifice of the wicked, but the prayer of the upright pleases him. Proverbs 15:8

He who ignores discipline despises himself, but whoever heeds correction gains understanding. Proverbs 15:32

A gift opens the way for the giver and ushers him into the presence of the great. Proverbs 16:23

A discerning man keeps wisdom in view, but a fool's eyes wander to the ends of the earth. Proverbs 17:24

Listen to advice, accept instruction, and in the end you will be wise. Proverbs 17:24

Many are the plans in a man's heart, but it is the LORD'S purpose that prevails. Proverbs 19:21

Be self-controlled and alert. Your enemy the devil prowls around like a roaring lion looking for someone to devour. Resist him, standing firm in the faith, because you know that your brother throughout the world are undergoing the same kind of sufferings. Peter 5:8 and 9

For the eyes of the LORD are on the righteous and his ears are attentive to their prayer, but the face of the LORD is against those who do evil. 1st Peter 1:10 and 11

Blessed is he whose transgressions are forgiven, whose sins are covered. Blessed is the man whose sin the LORD does not count against him and in whose spirit is not deceit. Psalms 32:1 and 2

I acknowledge my sin to you and did not cover up my iniquity. I will confess my transgressions to the LORD and HE forgave the guilt of my sin. Psalms 32:5

How priceless is GOD'S unfailing LOVE. Psalms 36:7

I have never seen the righteous forsaken or their children begging bread. They are always generous and lend freely; their children will be blessed. Proverbs 37:25 and 26

The angel of the LORD encamps around those who fear him and he delivers them. Psalms 34:7

Now to him who is able to do immeasurable more than all we ask or imagine, according to his power that is at work within us, to him be glory in the church and in CHRIST JESUS throughout all generations, for ever and ever! Amen. Ephesians 3:20

But when you pray, go into your room, close the door and pray to your FATHER, who sees what is done in secret, will reward you. Matthew 6:6

Ask and it will be given to you; seek and you will find; knock and the door will be opened to you. For everyone who ask receives; he who seeks finds; and to him who knocks the door will be opened. Matthew 7:7 and 8

It is not the healthy who need a doctor, but the sick, this means I desire mercy not sacrifice. For I have not come to call the righteous, but the sinners. Matthew 9:12 and 13

I tell you that if two of you on earth will agree about anything you ask for, it will be done for you by my father in heaven. For where two or three come together in my name, there am I with them. Matthew 18:19 and 20

Whoever lives by the truth comes into the LIGHT, so that it may be seen plainly that what he has done has been done through GOD. John 3:21

The thief comes only to steal, kill, and destroy; I have come that they may have life, and have it to the full. John 10:10

Cast all your anxiety on him because he cares for you. 1 Peter 5:7

For GOD did not give us the spirit of timidity, but a spirit of power, of love, and of self discipline. 2 Timothy 1:7

Don't you know that you yourselves are GOD'S temple and that GOD'S SPIRIT lives in you for GOD'S temple is sacred and you are that temple. 1st Corinthians 3:16 and 17

GOD made him who had no sin to be sin for us, so that in HIM we might become the righteous for GOD. 2 Corinthians 5:21

Examine yourselves to see whether you are in the faith; test yourselves. Do you not realize that CHRIST JESUS is in you-unless of course, you fail the test? And I trust that you will discover that we have not failed the test. 2 Corinthians 13:5

May GOD HIMSELF, the GOD OF PEACE, SANCTIFY you through and through. May your whole spirit, soul, and body be kept blameless at the coming of our LORD JESUS CHRIST. The one who calls you is faithful and he will do it. 1 Thessalonians 5:23 and 24

Stop sinning or something worse may happen to you. John 5:14

For the LORD watches over the ways of the righteous. Psalms 1:16

For death is the destiny of every man. Ecclesiastes 7:2

Printed in the United States
By Bookmasters